Writing the News

Writing

A GUIDE FOR

the News

PRINT JOURNALISTS

SECOND EDITION

Walter Fox

IOWA STATE UNIVERSITY PRESS / AMES

Walter Fox is Journalism Coordinator at West Chester University in Pennsylvania. A graduate of Columbia University's Graduate School of Journalism, Fox has more than 23 years of experience as a professional journalist, editor, communications specialist and journalism educator.

© 1993 Iowa State University Press, Ames, Iowa 50014
© 1977 Walter J. Fox, Jr.
Originally published by Hastings House, Publishers, Inc.

♾ Printed on acid-free paper in the United States of America

First edition, 1977
Second edition, 1993
    Through four printings
Paperback edition, 1998

Credits: pp. 33-34, news story from the *Chicago Tribune,* copyrighted © Jan. 4, 1992, Chicago Tribune Company, all rights reserved, used with permission. Pp. 38-39, 79-80, news stories from the Associated Press, used with permission. Pp. 44-45, 96-97, 132, 141-142, excerpts from news and feature stories from the *Los Angeles Times,* used with permission. Pp. 86-87, excerpt from news story from *The New York Times,* copyright © The New York Times Company, reprinted by permission. Pp. 91-92, news story from *The Post,* King of Prussia, Pa., used with permission. Pp. 109-110, excerpt from a copyrighted article in the *News Journal,* Wilmington, Del., used with permission. Pp. 131, 137-138, 139, 145, 150-151, excerpts from feature stories from *The Philadelphia Inquirer,* © 1988, 1991 *The Philadelphia Inquirer,* used with permission.

International Standard Book Number: 0-8138-2675-6 (pbk)

Library of Congress Cataloging-in-Publication Data

Fox, Walter
    Writing the news: a guide for print journalists / Walter Fox.—2nd. ed.
        p. cm.
    Includes bibliographical references and index.
    ISBN 0-8138-2675-6 (pbk. : alk. paper)
    1. Journalism—Authorship.   2. Report writing.   I. Title.
PN4783.F63   1998
808'.06607—dc21   97-44470

Last digit is the print number: 9 8 7 6 5 4 3 2 1

CONTENTS

PREFACE
TO THE SECOND EDITION

Much has happened—both in the world and in the American press—since this book was first published in 1977. Media today are reporting on the consequences of events barely imaginable less than two decades ago: the collapse of the Soviet Union and its satellite system in Eastern Europe, the worldwide menace of the AIDS virus, widespread drought and famine in Africa, the rise of Islamic fundamentalism and—here at home—a $300 billion savings and loan bailout and a $4 trillion national debt.

As journalists scramble to keep abreast of epochal events, their own profession continues to undergo radical alteration. Electronic media linked by satellite provide live news coverage from almost any spot on the globe. Computerized newsrooms coordinate every aspect of the newspaper production process from stories fed directly from the news scene by reporters with laptops to the makeup of entire pages on video display terminals. Electronic databases offer immediate access to whole categories of information.

Never before have journalists had at their disposal so much newsgathering technology. Yet, at some point, newspaper reporters must leave technology behind and *write* their stories. Here the skills of the writer come into play, and it is these skills—more than any others—that determine whether reporters will successfully communicate their findings to the reader. Poorly written and badly organized stories deter readers from gaining information that may be essential to their well-being. Editors committed to quality journalism place a premium on good writing when they set out to hire reporters.

Like the first edition, this book focuses on the newswriting process and describes the skills a beginning reporter needs to break into the profession. While this is the primary goal, I would hope that, along with practical advice, readers will take from the book an appreciation of the craft of newswriting as a modern art form—a writing style that has had an extraordinary impact on contemporary communications. To emphasize the vitality of the craft, I have placed it in a historical context, suggesting that the same forces which changed news style in the past still affect contemporary newspaper journalism.

If the reader should detect a slight bias in favor of print journalism, it is intentional. Without denying the power of electronic media or diminishing their important function as transmitters of news, I feel strongly that despite a somewhat lower profile than it once enjoyed, the newspaper continues to play a pivotal role in journalism.

Important news does not always have a visual dimension, nor is it necessarily connected to a specific event. It may contain no elements of violence or destruction; yet it is important because it is useful to people, because it enables them to take a greater degree of control over their lives or their environment, or because it allows them to see themselves and their community in relation to the larger society. The emphasis in electronic media—especially television—on "eyewitness" and "action" news, downgrades this kind of information in favor of stories with a more sensational impact on the viewer.

There never has been a superabundance of substantive news—probably because to produce it requires far more time and effort than reporting on homicides or fires—but when it appears, it is usually in a newspaper. Today's print journalists who attempt to provide it will need all the writing skills they can muster to attract readers accustomed to television's vivid imagery.

I would like to thank everyone who offered assistance or suggestions in preparing the second edition, but particularly the editors and manuscript committee at Iowa State University Press. This edition, as was the first, is dedicated to my wife, Francine, whose support and encouragement made the task a much less difficult one.

Writing the News

1 Writing for Newspapers

BEGINNING JOURNALISTS are often bewildered by the sheer number of rules they are asked to follow in constructing a news story, especially when these rules seem to contradict much of what they have learned about writing in composition classes.

They are told to order their information in a way that reverses the traditional method of telling a story. They are told to keep their words and sentences short, to write with verbs instead of adjectives and to ignore the rules for paragraphing. Then—while trying to keep all of these admonitions in mind—they are told they must finish the story in an unreasonably short period of time.

Is it any wonder that many journalism students suspect that the rules for newswriting are a kind of professional hazing process invented by editors and journalism professors?

The real culprits in this situation, however, are not so easily identified. Learning to write for newspapers is a process that demands considerable effort and concentration, but the rules for newspaper writing are an outgrowth of the requirements for communicating with an unseen audience through a unique print medium. They are not a set of arbitrary principles, nor are they engraved in stone. Instead, they have been evolving over the past 250 years in response to the changing technology of communications.

Stressing the power of technology to shape newswriting may not make it any easier for beginners to learn the craft, but it may render the process more understandable and much less frustrating. To point out that newswriting evolves in response to technological change is only another way of saying that it is a dynamic form of the written word—a form in close touch with the mood and tempo of human affairs.

It is no coincidence that an unusually large number of modern novelists, poets and playwrights have come from the ranks of newspaper reporters. The long list of journalistically trained writers stretches from Mark Twain, who was associated in some way with newspapers for 18 years of his career, to Kurt Vonnegut, who was a reporter at Chicago's City News Bureau after World War II. It includes Bret Harte, Stephen Crane, O. Henry, Theodore Dreiser, Sinclair Lewis, John O'Hara, Sherwood Anderson, Ernest Hemingway and John Hersey.

Both Walt Whitman and Carl Sandburg had considerable newspaper experience, and playwright Eugene O'Neill credited the publisher of a now-defunct Connecticut newspaper—where he worked briefly as a reporter—as the first person who "really thought I had something to say, and believed I could say it."

Even the relatively few writers who bypassed this experience have been forced to adapt their style to the lean, verb-oriented prose that has come to characterize newspaper writing. It would be no exaggeration to suggest that, without some familiarity with the rhetoric of journalism, a writer today has little hope of reaching a mass audience through the medium of print.

Early newspaper style

Newspaper readers in any era tend to assume that the writing they see in newspapers represents newspaper style and that this style passed on intact from one generation of journalists to another. This assumption is patently false, but only by tracing the development of newswriting from its beginnings on this continent in the early 1700s can the changes in news style and structure be observed.

The Colonial newspaper, as it existed along the Eastern seaboard, was a primitive operation by modern standards. Rarely larger than four letter-sized pages and issued once or twice a week, it was produced on a wooden handpress with hand-set type by a printer who did job work on the side. Reporting—as it is understood today—did not exist; printers used whatever news came into their shop or what they could glean from other newspapers, foreign and domestic.

Writing style varied from item to item within a single newspaper and from printer to printer, but with rare exceptions it was likely to be artless, colloquial and unsophisticated. Since it was assumed that subscribers would read the entire paper, there was no need to structure stories to arouse interest.

Typical of Colonial news style is the following story from a July 1704 issue of the *Boston News-Letter,* the first regularly published American newspaper:

> *Piscataqua, July, 6.* On Tuesday last eight Indians were seen at York, who had almost surpriz'd one *Shaw,* that was at some distance from the Garrison: The Indians were within pistol shot, and might have kill'd him, but striving still to surround & take him alive, (as supposed for Intelligence) he by that means, being a nimble active man, made his escape. Captain *Heath* & Lieutenant *March* immediately went in pursuit of them 6. or 7. Mils, but no discovery.

The first half of the 19th century saw considerable improvement in printing technology. Most newspaper printers were using iron presses that could produce a stronger and more even impression over a larger area of type. When combined with new and more legible type faces, this development made the newspaper of the day—usually four pages, tabloid size—a much more attractive and readable product. After 1833, enterprising "penny press" publishers hired reporters to go out and search for news.

But even with these advances, the news story continued to be rambling, obtuse and laced with political diatribe and moral indignation. Not until the late 1840s, when newspapers were linked to the telegraph wire, was there any real pressure to change the way news was written.

Structuring the news

The simple act of sending a news story by telegraph imposed a new discipline on newspaper reporters. Telegraph rates were high, service was subject to frequent interruptions and there was competition. It was not unusual at disaster scenes for a half dozen reporters to converge on a single telegraph operator, with each one demanding precedence on the wire. To avoid bloodshed, telegraphers adopted the practice of sending one paragraph of each reporter's story, in rotation, and then another, and so on.

Faced with the prospect of getting only one or two paragraphs to their respective papers before deadline, reporters made the first paragraph of their stories a complete summary of the news. Then, as they gained additional time on the wire, they would send more details but always in descending order of importance. By constructing stories with a news summary or "lead" at the beginning and minor details at the end, reporters protected themselves; regardless of where it might be interrupted by a break in communications or a newspaper deadline, their report was a comprehensible whole. Thus was born the "inverted pyramid" story—a staple of modern journalism and the bane of generations of newswriting students.

By the 1880s, the Associated Press was instructing its writers to tell all of the important facts in the first paragraph, and it was an AP correspondent, John P. Dunning, covering the disastrous Samoan hurricane of 1889, who wrote what became a classic lead of that era:

> Apia. Samoa, March 30. — The most violent and destructive hurricane ever known in the Southern Pacific passed over the Samoan Islands on the 16th and 17th of March, and as a result, a fleet of six warships and ten other vessels were ground to atoms on the coral reefs in the harbor, or thrown on the beach in front of the little city of Apia, and 142 officers and men of the American and German navies sleep forever under the reefs or lie buried in unmarked graves, thousands of miles from their native lands.

Although this lead would be considered excessively verbose by today's standards, Dunning had shown that a good writer could meet the demands of the telegraphic style and still convey the news in a dramatic and interesting manner.

At this point, the reader may ask, "Now that entire news stories can be transmitted instantaneously by fax, modem or satellite, why is it necessary to retain a structure built around an obsolete technology?" The answer is that a large part of the new journalistic environment ushered in by the telegraph is still with us.

The ratio of news to the space available for printing it is even higher today than it was when the problem was created by the telegraph. With all of this news moving at electric speed and its relative importance subject to instant change, stories constructed in a way that allows for drastic cutting without rewriting make the task much easier. Because it can be cut from the bottom up to meet space requirements, the inverted pyramid form is ideally suited to this purpose.

Today's newspapers—like the larger newspapers generated by the telegraph—create problems for readers who have neither the time nor the inclination to read every item. Inverted pyramid stories permit the reader to decide after scanning one paragraph whether to continue reading the story.

Finally, the inverted pyramid continues to serve the reporter, though no longer as insurance against a communications breakdown. By sharply reducing the transmission time of news, the telegraph heightened a growing fetish among newspapers for the "latest" news and put increasing pressure on reporters to write stories literally in a matter of minutes. What the inverted pyramid structure offers writers, who still face impossible deadlines, is a prefabricated story form on which to hang information in a relatively short time. Reporters who use it have the added security of knowing that if time runs out before they are done, only the least important material will be left out.

Stripped-down prose

"If telegraph shortened the sentence," Marshall McLuhan observed, "radio shortened the news story, and TV injected the interrogative mood into journalism."

The telegraph shortened sentences because transmission rates were based on the number of words. To reduce charges, reporters cut stories to the bone, often leaving out articles and other unnecessary words. These skeletonized reports would be fleshed out by editors at the receiving end; even so, the new technological pressure for brevity could not help but affect overall sentence length.

As important as it was in giving structure to the news story, the telegraph must share the honors for shaping news style with another 19th-century invention: the typewriter. Indifferent at first to the advantages of the typewriter, newspaper editors became interested—if not enthusiastic—after 1884 when Associated Press telegraph operators began using the contraption to produce clean, legible copy. After handling the neatly typed stories from the wire service, it was not long before editors ordered the machines for their own writers.

But the effects of the typewriter went far beyond cleaner and more readable copy. The typewriter, as McLuhan has pointed out, "fuses composition and publication, causing an entirely new attitude to the written or printed word." By composing on the typewriter, journalists became, in effect, publishers of their own writing. As their ideas flowed immediately into print, they became acutely aware of sentence structure, diction and the rhythm of words and phrases.

Forced by the typewriter to be both authors and critics of their own work, reporters soon discarded their wordy and colloquial style for the stripped-down prose that would become synonymous with newspaper journalism. It seemed almost as if the staccato movement of the machine had been transmitted to the writing it produced. Sentences shortened further and turned overwhelmingly to the active voice. Excess adjectives and adverbs were pruned to emphasize the verb. The lead took on a life of its own, with painstaking effort devoted to its construction.

This crisp new style reached its apex after 1913 as the wire services gradually changed over from the telegraph key and Morse code to the teletype, which combined the telegraph with the typewriter. The teletype provided newspapers with complete, typed stories that merely had to be ripped from the machines, edited for capitalization (the teletype used only capital letters) or cut, if necessary. With the increasing volume of wire copy flowing into newsrooms, it was far simpler for newspapers to adopt the style of the wire services than to make the wire copy conform to their own.

So it came about that in the first quarter of the 20th century, the press associations assumed responsibility for perfecting and polishing the news story. Since wire service stories would be relayed to all parts of the country, they had to be free of regional or idiomatic expressions. Consequently, in the process of trying to strike a national mean, the wire services unintentionally created it.

The typical wire service story followed the inverted pyramid structure with a summary lead and an elaboration of the major aspects of the event in order of importance. Less significant material was placed at the end, where it could be cut without damaging the story. Wire service copy was tightly written and marked by smooth transitions from paragraph to paragraph and the positioning of key words at the beginning of sentences to heighten interest.

This story, from the Associated Press in 1925, could serve as a classic example of the form at the peak of its development:

> NEW YORK, Feb. 5. — Praying, fasting and singing hymns, thirteen former Seventh Day Adventists on Long Island today are awaiting the end of the world.
>
> They think it will come tomorrow.
>
> They are led by Robert Reidt, who calls himself the "Apostle of Doom." The party includes men, women and children, and a family of four negroes.
>
> Most of them have sold their worldly goods, even part of their clothing, and are spending the last few days on carrots and water.
>
> Tomorrow they will go to a hill top near East Patchogue to hear the trumpet of doom. They expect to be taken in a cloud chariot to the woods near San Diego, Calif., where they say 144,000 "Brides of the Lamb" will be gathered.
>
> All other people will perish, according to their prediction.
>
> Announcement at headquarters of the Seventh Day Adventists at Washington that tomorrow is not the decreed date for the millennium has not affected the preparations of the little band.
>
> Mrs. Margaret W. Rowen, leader of those who have fixed the date for tomorrow, was denounced by the church leaders.
>
> It is the contention of the Adventist

organization that the date fixed by her is
extremely premature.

The Seven Plagues—including the Great
Battle of Armageddon—must come before
the world's doom, it is maintained by the
main group of Adventists.

But Reidt has made his predictions in
detail. The period of destruction, starting
tomorrow midnight, will last for seven days,
he says, with fire, disease, hailstones and
pestilence striking the earth at one time.

Reidt is himself no longer a member of the
Adventist Church. He has sold his furniture
to a second hand dealer on condition he may
buy it back.

The Apostle of Doom—a pale faced, fat
little man of thirty-three, with a buxom wife
and four pallid, frightened-looking children
between the ages of six and twelve—said he
had seen a vision in which he had been shown
how the messiah would appear to the faithful
and transport them to San Diego.

The wire service story form was copied by reporters all over the
country, occasionally to the detriment of more original writing at the
local level. Yet in the hands of a capable writer, it provided a sleek
and understated container for news.

The electronic revolution

Electromechanical inventions in the 19th century had broadened
the scope and enhanced the power of the daily newspaper, but the
electronic technology of the 20th century was not as friendly. It
challenged the communications monopoly of the press with wholly
new media of its own: first radio, then the newsreel and documentary
film and finally television. Thus, the continuing evolution of news
style after 1900 is primarily a response to external pressure.

Once radio stations began to offer spot news coverage, including
on-the-scene reports and interviews, print journalists faced a dilemma:
How should news be presented to readers who have already heard the
essential aspects of the story? The first response came from the newly
established tabloid newspapers, and that was to single out certain

stories and treat them in depth—both in words and pictures—and to condense and summarize the remaining news.

Despite the sensational nature of their subjects, tabloids perfected the news feature, a story form that combined hard news with the techniques of fiction for maximum impact. Even in their condensation of straight news, tabloids excelled in vivid writing that would be copied by the standard-sized dailies.

Another print response to radio was the appearance of the weekly newsmagazines—first *Time* in 1923, then *Newsweek* a decade later, and finally *U.S. News & World Report.* Like the tabloids, newsmagazines worked well in the altered media situation created by radio. Aimed at what *Time* described as the "busy" reader, newsmagazines presented major foreign and national news in well-written and entertaining summaries.

In their writing style, newsmagazines went even further than the tabloids in departing from the standard news story structure. To give zest to news that often was a week old and already known in its essentials to readers, newsmagazines turned back to the old narrative form but in a smooth and sophisticated manner and with a strong undercurrent of human interest. *Time*'s stated intention of making all of its copy appear to have been written by one author was carried out, to the disdain of critics who dubbed the inverted sentence structure and telescoped modifiers "*Time* style."

Newsmagazine style had little effect on newspaper writing, although a much less stylized version of the narrative form could be seen in the growing number of Sunday newspaper sections that reviewed the week's news. Nevertheless, it was becoming increasingly clear that newspaper readers who had heard the *Hindenburg* zeppelin disaster on radio live from Lakehurst, N.J., and who had listened to Edward R. Murrow's broadcasts during the bombing of London in World War II, would come to expect more from print media than a standardized news story.

INTERPRETATIVE NEWS

Radio's ability to take listeners to the scene of news events or to bring the voices of world leaders into their living rooms was the most obvious reason for the immediate popularity of the new medium. Less apparent, but possibly more significant from a journalistic standpoint, was that radio was creating a seamless web of instantaneous communication covering the entire planet. By virtue of this fact, all news would now have a global dimension. It was no longer adequate for reporters simply to furnish a factual account of *what* had happened; of the traditional "five W's" of reporting, the *why* suddenly became paramount. In the electronic age, news needed meaning and context, and the task of providing these took on a special name: *interpretation.*

Radio moved quickly to supply news analysis, and—despite the inherent limitations of its broadcast format for in-depth reporting—produced an array of commentators who combined a compelling oral delivery with perceptive insights on current events. Newspapers, wedded to the concept of "objectivity," were reluctant to take the plunge even though the print medium was ideal for the interpretative role. Editors trained in preradio journalism resisted the new movement to interpretation almost as much as they resisted the new medium itself. For a time, the general unwillingness of the daily press to adapt to the new media situation allowed newsmagazines, journals of opinion and radio to monopolize news analysis by default.

Complex events leading up to World War II, including the civil war in Spain, put enormous pressure on daily newspapers to provide some explanation for the chaotic events in Europe. Consequently, foreign correspondents were given a free hand to incorporate their own observations and judgments into news stories. But back home, a reporter covering city hall under the watchful eye of an old-school editor had to bootleg such information, attributing it to "informed sources."

Not until the 1960s, with the daily press scrambling for survival in the wake of television, did newspapers begin to seriously experiment with a more meaningful presentation of news. This experimentation took two forms: an interest in stories that offered readers a meaningful context for the events they were witnessing on TV, and an attempt to create a more attractive visual package for news. The former resulted in longer stories that blended feature techniques with news reporting and analysis; the latter, in a more coherent graphic display combining modern typography, photography and modular layout. It would be another decade, however, until the surviving dailies, goaded by the revelations of the underground press and muckraking magazines, would fully embrace interpretation as a matter of policy.

THE ELECTRONIC NEWSROOM

Viewed for more than a half century as a competitor, electronic technology finally entered the newsroom in the 1970s as newspaper publishers began to install computerized editing systems that required reporters to write their stories at video display terminals (VDTs)—keyboards with monitors linked to a mainframe computer. In such an environment, news can be written, edited, stored and typeset from within the computer system and sent or imported by satellite or telephone wire to and from other systems.

The initial discomfort that accompanies any radical shift in technology was soon forgotten as newspaper journalists realized how easily stories could be revamped, edited and polished—even under deadline conditions. For writers, the VDT combines the benefits of the typewriter and computer to provide maximum control over the structure of sentences and the shape of the story. If good writing is rewriting, composition on a screen makes that process as painless as possible; all constructions are tentative and can be altered at the touch of a key.

Editors who have worked under both systems are nearly unanimous in claiming that the electronic newsroom has raised the overall quality of newspaper writing. Some note, however, that while factual accuracy has increased largely due to the ease with which corrections can be made right up to deadline, the number of typographical errors also has increased because news copy is seen by fewer editors.

The rest of the story is current history. Electronic technology has ushered in a new era of print journalism marked by a great diversity of style and structure, as well as by the flowering of new journalistic forms. No longer is the word "journalism" synonymous with the daily press, as it was in the 1920s. Today it includes—along with radio and television news operations—local and national weeklies; news-magazines; specialized news services; city and regional magazines; racial, ethnic and tribal newspapers; and independent publications serving vocational and professional groups.

Yet the present is built on the past. The great legacy of the daily newspaper era has been the development of a clear prose style, free not only of idiom and colloquialism but also of the literary and moral cant that marred so much of 19th-century writing. Today's journalistic language is a kind of tempered English, a vigorous, disciplined prose forged in the Industrial Revolution and hardened in nearly a century of international conflict. It remains the most flexible and adaptable form of English and one that, in a new age, may just as effectively serve the cause of peace. It is this language—its structure and its style—that will be examined in the following chapters.

2 Writing the Lead

WHEN USED for newsgathering, the telegraph completely reshaped the news story, placing extreme emphasis on the first paragraph or "lead," as journalists call it. In the early days of the telegraph style, the lead was expected to be a complete summary of the story with enough details for it to stand alone if a deadline made that necessary.

Even a brief examination of today's newspapers will indicate how far lead writing style has evolved since the 19th century. Styles may have changed drastically in a hundred years, but the ability to construct a good lead remains the newswriter's most important task.

The reader is likely to ask, "What is a good lead?" While the answer will vary in its specifics, depending on the type of story being written, a fundamental rule can be applied to all lead writing: An effective lead is one that will catch the reader's attention *honestly* and direct it to what the writer feels is the essential point or news angle of the story.

Lead writing, thus, is a two-step process. The first step is to distill from a mass of facts, figures and quotations the single coherent statement that—in the writer's view—best expresses the meaning of the story. The second is to write this statement in a way that will have maximum impact on the reader.

Since the first step involves value judgments made by the writer on the facts, it does not lie entirely within the province of journalism. It is affected to a considerable degree by the writer's maturity and experience, both as a reporter and as a human being. It is also relative to the context of the story and the readership for which it is intended.

For all of these reasons, the ability to extract lead statements is not easily learned or taught in school. It is best acquired working for a newspaper or, at least, in a situation that closely approximates actual newspaper reporting. *Writing* the lead, however, is a purely journalistic function, and while a writer may spend a lifetime trying out new devices, there are a few basic rules that—once mastered—can be used with maximum effect even by beginners.

For the sake of order, lead writing will be examined from two distinct aspects, structure and language.

Lead structure

Nowhere can the effect of electronic media on the news story be seen as easily as in the structure of the lead paragraph. In the heyday of the telegraphic style, from the late 1880s to the 1920s, the lead paragraph was a story in miniature, often consisting of two or three fact-filled sentences. The following lead, taken from *The New York Times* in 1890, is fairly typical of the period:

> DANBURY, Conn., Feb. 2. — This city suffered the most disastrous fire in its history this morning. It consumed a half dozen large buildings and several minor structures in the very heart of the business district, Main and Liberty streets, and cleaned out many of the largest retail establishments, besides a half hundred or more offices and over four hundred people occupying tenements in the blocks. The total loss will be something over $300,000, the bulk of which falls on Charles Hull, representing the Hull estate.

Leads were written this way not out of ignorance or a lack of sophistication but simply because they had to be. News flowed through the telegraph wire, and for a major story to overcome the numerous obstacles to transmission, not to mention newspaper deadlines, the story had to be constructed in self-contained units. Even if no further information were received by the newspaper, the lead could stand by itself as a front-page bulletin.

With the arrival of radio in the 1920s as an alternative news medium, the pressure on the telegraph newspaper began to ease, and while leads continued to be long—almost always two sentences—there was a perceptible decline in the number of facts included. Lead writing at this time began a gradual movement towards the uncluttered contemporary style.

Such a shift is evident by 1926 as this example from the Philadelphia *Public Ledger* indicates:

> Samuel Holt, paymaster of Armour & Co., was slain by payroll bandits yesterday afternoon at 11th and Noble Sts. Caught between a crossfire of lead, he slumped to the floor of his automobile, riddled with bullets.

Radio had broken the absolute domination of the five W's—who, what, when, where, and why. Readers who had heard a news bulletin on the radio were not interested in a simple repetition of the facts; they wanted an explanation. Thus, it was pressure from radio that raised to new prominence the often neglected *why* in newspaper lead writing. As radio moved strongly into news coverage during World War II, newswriters became more selective in composing leads, using only those "W's" they felt were really necessary to the story. The others would be held for later paragraphs.

READABILITY AND NEWS

After the war, the wire services, which were becoming more acutely aware of the shift in story values, hired readability experts to study their copy and make recommendations. One of these experts, Dr. Rudolph Flesch, had developed a formula for measuring readability, which determined the most readable writing to be made up of words averaging 1.5 syllables and sentences averaging no more than 19 words. Acting on his advice, the Associated Press succeeded in reducing its average lead sentence length from 27 to 23 words and its word length in leads from 1.74 to 1.55 syllables.

Another expert, Robert Gunning, who was retained by the United Press, reached similar conclusions and developed what he called a "fog index" to measure the complexity of writing. By applying the Gunning index, the UP simplified its writing style so that it would be understood by readers with 11.7 years of education. The wire service formerly had been writing at a level suitable for readers with 16.7 years of education, according to Gunning.

The attempt to apply a scientific yardstick to a craft as imprecise and flexible as newswriting drew sharp criticism from many journalists who felt that readability formulas were, in effect, a stylistic straitjacket. But the wire services were able to make their own writers conform at least to the general recommendations of the experts, and the simplified copy emanating from teletypes in hundreds of city rooms across the country ultimately had considerable impact on newspaper style.

If the readability experts failed in the long run to obtain a universal acceptance of their formulas, they did succeed in forcing journalists to look much more closely at their own writing in terms of clarity and readability. In this process, newspaper style was improved.

STREAMLINED LEADS

The emphasis on readability, combined with the increasing pressure of electronic journalism, had produced by the end of the 1950s a streamlined lead consisting of a single sentence, usually less than 25 words in length, that played up only the most important elements of the story. This lead from the Philadelphia *Evening Bulletin* in 1954 is typical of the crisp new style that would prevail in daily newspapers right up to the present:

> The much-debated charter amendments
> today appeared headed for a floor fight in
> City Council.

Today when editors talk about lead writing, they mean the ability to construct a single emphatic sentence that conveys the essential elements of a given story. Clearly, a story is selected for publication because the editors believe it is important or of interest to a large number of readers. The selection process may take into account such considerations as timeliness, proximity, prominence of the subjects, impact on the community and appeal to human interest.

Which news elements are essential in the lead and which are not will depend to some degree on several factors, among them the nature of the publication and whether it is issued daily or weekly. Geographic and regional concerns also come into play and, ultimately, the specific readership to which the paper is directed.

In certain categories of news stories, such as accidents, fires, and disasters, there is a longstanding consensus among journalists that death and injury to victims must be spelled out in the lead. In stories dealing with property damage or financial loss, an estimate of the monetary value of the damage or loss should be part of the lead. Beyond these special kinds of stories, the decision as to what must be included is made by the writer within the context of his or her publication.

The concern in this chapter is not so much what must be included as, having decided what to include, how to express it as emphatically as possible in one sentence. It is at this point that newswriting instruction veers away from English composition as it is traditionally taught. Unlike the first sentence of most themes, the lead of a news story is *not* a preface. It does not lead up to the story or prepare the reader for what is to come. In newswriting, the lead *is* the story!

Constructing an effective lead, therefore, requires the writer to confront the whole story at the outset in some meaningful way. For most beginners in newswriting, this is the greatest obstacle they will have to overcome, since it stands in direct opposition to writing habits acquired over the years in composition classes. But it is a technique that must be mastered since it is a fundamental skill of journalism.

Aside from its role in conveying the essence of a news story, the lead also determines to a large extent the shape and tone of the material that will follow. So close is this relationship that it is difficult, if not impossible, to write a good story under a poorly constructed lead. Thus, the inordinate amount of time and effort most journalists put into lead writing pays off later in the form of a smoothly flowing story.

Lead language

At the beginning of this chapter, a lead was described not simply as a sentence but as an *emphatic* sentence. This means that the lead must be constructed to obtain maximum impact for the ideas expressed. To achieve impact, journalists draw upon all of the traditional emphatic devices of the English language, but some they adapt to their own purposes. In lead writing, the most useful techniques for gaining emphasis are word order, voice, verb selection, subordination and coordination.

WORD ORDER

In composition classes, students learn that the most emphatic parts of a sentence are the beginning and the end. But since climactic order is usually stressed, the end takes precedence as the most emphatic position.

On a newspaper page, however, every story directly competes with every other story for the reader's attention, and to hold back key information until the end of the lead might lose potential readers. At least, that is the theory. Whether it really happens or not is a moot question. Writers have been constructing leads on the basis of this theory for so long that newspaper readers are trained to expect the most important element to appear at the beginning.

Thus, for lead writing, the old composition dictum is reversed: The beginning of the sentence is the most emphatic, and the end next in emphasis. The middle, as always, is reserved for material to be de-emphasized.

In the following lead from the *Philadelphia Inquirer,* the writer has decided that the "why" is the most significant aspect of the news and has placed it at the front of the sentence:

> Lax practices in hospitals and outpatient clinics are contributing to the spread of new strains of tuberculosis resistant to traditional drug treatment, scientists warned yesterday.

It would have been just as easy to write:

> New strains of tuberculosis resistant to traditional drug treatment are being spread by

> lax practices in hospitals and outpatient
> clinics, scientists warned yesterday.

But this lead lacks emphasis because the key element has been buried in the middle of the sentence.

There is, however, one fairly common exception to this rule, and it is made when the writer feels that the key element of the lead would be more meaningful to the reader if placed in a wider context. To do this, the writer use a subordinate phrase or clause to introduce the main idea, as in this lead from the Associated Press:

> CHANTILLY, Va. — After 10 days of meet-
> ings, an international effort to forge a treaty
> on global warming has resulted in only an
> agreement on the number of committees to
> work on the issue and on the need for another
> session.

A corollary of the rule that key elements go first is to avoid cluttering the opening of the lead sentence with unimportant or meaningless words or phrases. Strong leads usually begin with names or nouns, rarely with prepositions and participles. Articles can be dropped when they do not aid meaning. Useless phrases, such as "in order to" (means "to"), "due to the fact that" (means "because") or "for the purpose of" (means "for") should be eliminated wherever they occur, even if it means rewriting the entire sentence.

VOICE

Since the active voice of verbs is ordinarily stronger and more emphatic than the passive, newswriters prefer it especially in constructing leads.

It is much more emphatic to write

> A car that ran out of control on Main
> Street early today damaged three parked
> vehicles before coming to rest in the window
> of a dress shop near 17th Street.

than to use the passive voice:

> Three parked vehicles and a storefront
> were damaged early today by a car that ran
> out of control on Main Street near 17th.

This general rule must immediately be qualified by pointing out that in many instances the passive is the more natural and emphatic form. When the receiver of the action is more significant than the doer, use of the passive voice permits writers to put that element at the beginning of the sentence, which is the most emphatic position.

> WINDOW ROCK, Ariz.—Peter McDonald, a former chairman of the Navajo tribe, was sentenced yesterday to 450 days in jail for bribery, fraud, conspiracy and ethics violations in the tribe's purchase of a ranch.

In the above lead from the Associated Press, the writer has correctly used the passive voice to emphasize the person who was sentenced, which is the significant news, rather than to begin with the name of the judge.

After some experience in writing leads, beginning journalists will find that the choice between active and passive verb forms becomes almost subconscious, determined largely by what element of the lead they wish to emphasize.

A more common problem, even among experienced newswriters, is a tendency to use passive verb forms rather than a single, active verb. Unless writers keep a critical eye on their own prose, they are likely to slip into a lead like this:

> After months of unsuccessful attempts to sell a controversial tax package to Greensburg residents, City Manager Frank Gibson submitted his resignation today to City Council.

It would be more emphatic in this instance to move the news angle to the front of the sentence and to simplify the verb:

> City Manager Frank Gibson resigned today after months of unsuccessful attempts to sell a controversial tax package to Greensburg residents.

All vague and passive verb forms, such as "gave consideration to," "took into custody" or "was the recipient of," should be discarded in favor of the single, active verb: "considered," "arrested," etc.

VERB SELECTION

The one element that distinguishes a living sentence from a static group of words is a strong verb. No adjective, however carefully chosen, can make up for the loss of emphasis caused by a weak or poorly chosen verb.

The reason for this lies in the nature of language itself. In any sentence the verb sets all of the other parts in motion. By selecting vigorous, descriptive verbs, writers provide the highest possible acceleration for the sentence and the maximum impact for the ideas it conveys.

Newswriting practice, with an eye to space limitations, has always stressed the importance of strong verbs, especially in leads. But even if space were not an issue, the key to vigorous writing lies in the careful selection of verbs.

Here a writer attempts to describe a fire by using an adjective:

> A raging fire, fanned by heavy winds, was out of control for more than five hours last night at an abandoned warehouse at 11th and Main streets.

The intended effect is dissipated by the use of "was," a form of the verb "to be"—the weakest verb in the language. By simply moving the description into the verb, the writer could increase the impact of the lead:

> A fire, fanned by heavy winds, *raged* out of control for more than five hours last night . . .

Effective newswriting uses verbs that tell not only what happened but also *how* it happened. Good writers would say that traffic "choked" rather than "filled" the downtown area, that hail storms "ravaged" rather than "destroyed" crops, or that striking transit workers "shouted down" rather than "rejected" a proposed settlement.

In each case, the verb arouses a sensory response in the reader.

To obtain this effect, however, writers cannot go beyond the facts of the story. Use of the verb "shouted down" implies that an emotional voice vote was taken by the strikers. The verb "ravaged" suggests violent and widespread damage. In the search for the telling verb, accuracy remains the final criterion.

SUBORDINATION AND COORDINATION

An examination of news leads according to sentence structure will show that most leads are complex sentences—that is, sentences which contain an independent and a dependent clause. Use of this structure sends a subliminal message to the reader: The independent clause is more important than the dependent clause.

What the term "subordination" means, when applied to lead writing, is that the writer should take pains to avoid frustrating the natural hierarchy of the sentence. To put it another way, the writer must place the news angle of the lead in the main clause of the sentence and the lesser aspects of the story in subordinate clauses.

Violations of this rule produce unemphatic and distorted leads, such as this one:

> City Manager Frank Gibson charged Greensburg Council members with "self interest" and "political cowardice" when he resigned yesterday.

This lead is perplexing. "Has Gibson really resigned?" the reader asks, then goes back and reads the sentence again.

The problem here is that important news has been placed in a subordinate clause and, consequently, de-emphasized, while less important material is given top billing. Confusion could have been eliminated by keeping the primary news angle in the main clause:

> City Manager Frank Gibson resigned yesterday, charging Greensburg Council members with "self-interest" and "political cowardice."

Any lead that must be read twice for understanding is a poor one.

In this long but effective lead from the *Philadelphia Inquirer,* the news is stated simply in the main clause, with a subordinate clause added to give readers the full significance of the item:

> WASHINGTON — Congress has approved the most expensive taxpayer bailout in history, a bill to spend $306 billion over more than 30 years rescuing the savings and loan industry from a financial disaster created largely by deliberate fraud.

As noted earlier, most news leads are complex sentences containing an independent and a dependent clause. This works well because most news stories are based on a single news element or incident. In less frequent cases where two or more important news elements belong in the lead, a different structure must be used.

To structure such a lead, the writer can choose a compound sentence with two or more independent clauses. Compound sentences are coordinating devices; they signal the reader that the thoughts contained are of equal importance.

In the following story from *The Washington Post,* the writer decided that two aspects of the story belonged in the lead and constructed a compound sentence to give both elements equal emphasis:

> LOS ANGELES — In response to the worst drought in California history, Gov. Pete Wilson yesterday named an emergency task force to deal with the critical water shortage and Los Angeles Mayor Tom Bradley called for mandatory water rationing in the city.

In this example from the Associated Press, a compound structure serves to contrast two important findings of a study:

> ATLANTA — More Americans are quitting smoking, but more are dying from smoking-related illnesses—nearly 450,000 a year—as the habits of the 1950s and '60s take an increasing toll, federal officials said yesterday.

By keeping key information at the front of the sentence,

maintaining active voice, choosing strong verbs and shaping the sentence to fit the news angle, writers maximize their ability to construct an emphatic lead.

Other considerations in lead writing

Up to this point, emphasis has been placed on the essential requirements for writing vigorous, emphatic news leads. Some occasions, however, require more—or at least a variation of the basic rules.

Every issue of a newspaper contains stories that, while weak in news value or social significance, more than make up for this shortcoming in humor, irony or human interest appeal. Such stories require special treatment and will be discussed in a later chapter.

Apart from considerations of style and emphasis, certain technical problems also arise in the writing of leads from the fundamental requirement that newswriting be clear and accurate. Most of these problems fall into two general areas: attribution and identification.

ATTRIBUTION

An examination of leads in almost any newspaper will turn up statements that simply would not be news unless made by an authoritative source, as in this example from *The New York Times:*

> SOUTH BEND, Ind., June 18 — A Gallup poll released here today finds that two-thirds of American Catholics favor opening the priesthood to women, an increase of 20 percentage points over just seven years ago.

A street-corner evangelist preaching the imminent destruction of the world will not send reporters running to their keyboards. But should a geophysicist studying the ozone layer reach a similar conclusion, his comments will be picked up by wire services and relayed from coast to coast. This phenomenon may only reflect the public's current preference for scientific rather than religious sources, but it underscores the fact that the statement itself, without a *recognized* authority behind it, fails to meet the test of news.

The journalist's specific task, then, is to determine which stories require this authority to be newsworthy and which do not and to write leads accordingly. Linking the newsworthy statement to an authority is called *attribution.*

In most cases, a generic identification rather than a proper name will provide the necessary attribution in the lead:

> Optimistic business forecasts by the President's Council of Economic Advisers were sharply disputed yesterday by a Harvard Business School economist.

Here, a general description of the authority is perfectly adequate to support the lead statement. The economist's name, which would not be familiar to most readers anyway, can be used in the second or third paragraph. In stories based on statistics or authoritative statements, good practice normally dictates that the writer include the source's proper name in the lead, as in this example from the Associated Press:

> WASHINGTON — Bilingual education programs help Spanish-speaking children excel in school, according to a study released yesterday by the Education Department.

Or in this from the *Philadelphia Inquirer:*

> WASHINGTON — The National Transportation Safety Board yesterday warned that handles on rear emergency exits on DC–9 and MD–80 jetliners could have "serious deficiencies" and called for immediate inspections and repairs, if necessary.

In the first example, the Education Department is the most authoritative source for the statement and should, therefore, be identified. Note that attribution comes at the end of the sentence, giving prime emphasis to the findings. In the second example, the authority, in effect, makes the news: The agency responsible for the safety of public carriers is calling attention to a possibly unsafe condition on certain aircraft. Thus, the name moves to the front of the lead.

Reporters covering public affairs—in city hall or at the White House—frequently obtain important stories from officials who, for one reason or another, cannot be identified. If the source is considered to be trustworthy, the reporter will use the story and attribute it in the lead to "an informed source" or "a high official."

The mechanics of attribution—how it is handled in direct quotation and paraphrasing—will be discussed in a later chapter.

IDENTIFICATION

Another technical problem related to the process of lead writing is identification. Simply stated, the problem is how does the writer identify each person, place or organization mentioned in the lead so that its connection with the news is immediately apparent to the reader?

At first glance, this might seem a minor concern. But when it is done poorly or not at all, the story suffers and readers find themselves asking, "I wonder if that's the same John Bradley who . . . ?"

Adequate identification is always relative to the subject's degree of prominence and, in some instances, to past prominence, of which the reading public may no longer be aware. In the latter case, it becomes the duty of the reporter to refresh the public memory.

Take for example an ordinary traffic accident in which the victim, Richard Williams, is critically injured. To identify the man in the lead simply as "Richard Williams" would be inadequate, since in the newspaper's circulation area there may be a dozen or more men named Richard Williams.

The only way to adequately identify the victim would be to include his full name with middle initial—if obtainable—his age and home address. Thus, his basic newspaper identity becomes Richard A. Williams, 57, of the 2200 block of Chestnut St. All three elements must appear as a unit, not separately inserted into the story.

If, in checking out the story, the reporter discovers that Williams is a well-known trial lawyer and a former district attorney, this degree of prominence requires that Williams be identified in the lead in the way most readers know him. The story, then, would begin:

> Richard A. Williams, a widely known trial lawyer and a former Philadelphia district attorney, was critically injured last night when he was struck by a car near 7th and Walnut streets.

While the subject's age and home address should appear in the story, that information is no longer crucial to identity.

The business of identification becomes more complex when dealing with people who are prominent in more than one sphere of activity. An actress who champions political and social causes, a businessman who is equally well-known as a civic leader, or a scholar whose expertise spans several areas of learning—all present problems for the lead writer.

To identify a multifaceted personality in one phrase requires singling out two or three of the subject's best-known areas of activity and holding back others for later in the story. The problem becomes most acute in writing leads for obituaries where a lifetime of activity must be summed up in a single phrase. In other kinds of writing, however, the nature of the story determines which attributes the writer features in the lead.

For the sake of illustration, suppose that a local environmental organization issues a news release announcing a forthcoming lecture on the subject of ocean pollution. The lecturer is a man who has been a chemist, marine biologist, diver and underwater explorer and an author of several books on environmental subjects. If one of those books has been widely publicized, the lead might read:

> Roger Anderson, marine biologist and author of "The Silent Sea," will speak on the threat of ocean pollution at . . .

If, instead, his books were all of a technical nature, the lead might begin:

> Roger Anderson, marine biologist and underwater explorer, will speak on . . .

By using a compound identification, the writer implies that Anderson's authority as a lecturer stretches beyond that of a scientific specialist—which, of course, is true. In either case, any relevant background not used in the lead would be inserted later in the story.

When preparing a story that follows up an earlier news account, the writer should identify the persons involved in terms of the previous story:

> James Dean, an 8-year-old Greensburg boy who was critically injured April 5 in a freak playground accident, died today at Memorial Hospital.

To identify the boy as "James Dean, 8, son of Mr. and Mrs. Edward F. Dean, 121 E. Elm St." would obscure the news, which is not that an 8-year-old boy died, but that *the boy who was injured at the playground two weeks ago* died. People who read the earlier story are likely to remember the incident but not the name of the victim.

In some stories, the subject's connection to a newsworthy event is even more important than his or her name, as in the following example from the Associated Press:

> LOS ANGELES — The only FBI agent ever convicted of espionage was sentenced to 20 years in prison yesterday by a judge who suggested that the agency should not have placed such an inept agent in control of sensitive documents.

Organizations whose names give no indication of their function also should be adequately identified in the lead. It is almost meaningless to write:

> James McDonnell, an area real estate broker, has been elected president of the Citizens Action Committee.

The news comes into focus only when the organization is properly identified as "a group vehemently opposed to public housing."

In dealing with persons, places or organizations, effective identification describes the subject in such a way that the reader can quickly establish its relationship to the news.

3 Developing the Story

WRITERS WHO CAN construct a lead sentence that simply and emphatically expresses the most important aspects of the news find themselves already one jump ahead in the process of developing the story. If the lead brings the news into sharp focus, the rest of the story seems to flow naturally from it.

A well-constructed lead provides the writer with a basic plan for developing the story. If the most important aspect of the story appears in the main clause and less important information is in the subordinate clause, the writer simply follows that order. Yet many beginners start to waver at precisely this point. Having written an acceptable lead, they tend to fall back on organizational devices learned in composition classes, such as chronological or climactic order.

In newswriting, the organizational method that applies to the story as a whole also applies to each part of the story, and that method is *order of importance.* The same critical stance that enables a writer to scan all of his or her material and construct an effective lead must be maintained throughout the story. Thus, the development of the lead begins with the most important part of the lead.

In the last chapter the following lead illustrated the principle of subordination:

> City Manager Frank Gibson resigned to-
> day, charging Greensburg Council members
> with "self-interest" and "political cowardice."

This lead spotlights the key aspect of the story in the main clause. The next task, then, is to develop the major news. If the lead emphasis is accurate, elaboration begins with the material in the main clause.

In the story at hand, this means that the circumstances of Gibson's resignation must be explained first and then his comments about city officials. Thus, the second paragraph of this story might read like this:

> Gibson announced his resignation during
> a hastily arranged press conference at City
> Hall. Speaking to reporters, he explained his
> action by reading from a letter he had sent to
> City Council.

Having amplified the fact of the resignation, the writer now moves on to the substance of Gibson's remarks—first dealing with the comments that were quoted briefly in the lead. The reader deserves an explanation of Gibson's attack on council, so the story might continue in this fashion:

> In his letter of resignation, Gibson said he
> had "labored unceasingly for more than a
> year to do those things that must be done to
> give the city a sound fiscal structure."
> "I was blocked at every turn by council
> members who placed their own self-interest
> above the good of the city," he said. "In 24
> years of public service I have rarely seen
> political cowardice so widespread in one
> legislative body."
> Gibson was referring to his failure to
> obtain the support of a majority of council
> members for a controversial tax package that
> he had repeatedly described as essential for
> the economic health of the city.
> The tax package would have included a
> new 5 percent sales tax on nonfood items and
> a 3 mill increase in the city's real estate tax
> rate.

At this point in the story the expectations of the reader that were aroused by the lead have been satisfied. Now the reporter can turn to other remarks of interest Gibson made at his press conference. Again, order of importance continues to be the rule, not the order in which Gibson made the comments:

> Gibson warned that Greensburg faced a bleak future unless residents were willing to confront its problems honestly and demand that their elected representatives take action.
>
> "The future of Greensburg now rests in the hands of its citizens," he declared. "If they are willing to rise above their own petty concerns and demand nothing less from their council members, there is no reason why the problems of this city cannot be surmounted."
>
> Gibson said his resignation would be effective April 1—one month from the date of his letter to council.
>
> He said he planned to take a two-week vacation in the Bahamas before making any plans for the future, but he disclosed that he was considering several offers of employment from municipalities along the Eastern Seaboard.

The story might also include background information on Gibson: when he was appointed, what he had done before coming to Greensburg, his professional credentials, etc. It might contain reactions to the resignation by council members, if they could be obtained. Regardless of what material is included, the story must be ordered consciously and continually along a descending spiral of importance that flows directly from the lead.

This story by *Chicago Tribune* writer John W. Fountain is a classic example of inverted pyramid development:

> One man has been arrested and another is being sought in connection with the robbery and slaying of a Hoffman Estates man whose body was found dumped in a brushy area near the Mississippi River.
>
> The body of Marc Crawford, 30, was discovered the morning of Dec. 27 about 20

feet from the Mississippi, one mile from Quincy.

Randy Schlueter, 21, of Quincy, has been charged with concealing a homicide. He was being held in the Adams County Jail on $50,000 bond, Adams County Sheriff Robert Nall said.

Schlueter had not been charged with murder as of late Friday, and authorities would not say whether he witnessed the slaying. But Nall said, "You can assume that he played a part in it."

Police were searching Friday for a second suspect believed to have played a role in the slaying. His identity was not released, although authorities said he was a young man who also lives in Quincy.

Authorities said they believe Crawford met the two young men near Irene's Cabaret, a bar in downtown Quincy, the night before he was killed.

"They had just come out of a nightclub and were in an alley when [Crawford] came by and asked them to go for a ride," Nall said.

Sometime after that, the men allegedly beat Crawford to death and took an undisclosed amount of cash and his wallet, Nall said.

Schlueter has been questioned by police and has helped provide some of the missing pieces to the Crawford murder, "pertinent information that directly relates to the case," Nall said.

Police would not disclose the type of weapon used in Crawford's death. They said the weapon was recovered late Thursday close to where Crawford's rental car was found, four miles from where the body was discovered.

Authorities earlier reported that a blunt object appeared to have been the weapon. A preliminary autopsy report released Friday showed that Crawford died of head wounds, Nall said.

Good development is never an easy task since it requires the writer to make value judgments all through the story. Certain types of stories require extra vigilance. In covering speeches by prominent personalities, writers often will be tempted to follow the speaker's order. They must resist this temptation by reminding themselves that they are writing for the newspaper's audience, not the speaker's.

In covering meetings of municipal bodies, where many unrelated actions are likely to occur, writers can easily slip back into chronological order after developing the lead. In such stories, each separate topic must be treated as an inverted pyramid story in itself, with its own lead and development.

Chronology has its place in newswriting. At times a chronology of events may be essential to the understanding of a story, but even in these cases chronology serves as merely a part of the story, not an ordering device.

Secondary leads

Most of the spot news stories that a journalist writes focus on a single incident and follow the pattern outlined above. Occasionally, reporters confront stories in which two or more key aspects should be featured in the lead. These stories call for a special kind of development that will be discussed in Chapter 6.

In other situations, a writer's obligation to provide readers with important information early in the story forces him or her to delay normal development of the main clause of the lead. Such situations occur whenever a writer feels that certain information, while not important enough to go into the lead sentence, is too newsworthy to hold until that point in the story where it would normally appear. In these instances the writer puts the relevant information in a "secondary lead," a paragraph immediately following the lead.

In the report of a legislative session, for instance, a secondary lead might sum up other pertinent actions not described in the lead. In stories based on statistics, it might cite exceptions to overall trends. In any event, a secondary lead breaks the normal development of the story, but serves readers' interest by acquainting them at the outset with the major aspects of the news. An example from the *Philadelphia Inquirer* illustrates this device:

> Asians, Hispanics and blacks accounted
> for nearly all of the population growth in the

> Philadelphia metropolitan area in the 1980s, according to U.S. Census Bureau numbers released yesterday.
>
> The white population in the eight counties barely grew at all—adding less than 14,000 to the area's total 1990 population of 4,856,881, according to the census bureau.
>
> By contrast, the area's Asian population more than doubled, and there was a 50 percent growth in the Hispanic population. The black population of the eight-county area rose 5 percent, or 45,502.

In the above example, the information in the third paragraph flows naturally from the lead sentence, but the author—judging the material in the second paragraph too important to wait until later—interrupts the normal flow of the story to make it a secondary lead. In other cases, the second paragraph of the story offers background material or historical data necessary for a full understanding of the lead, as in this *Washington Post* story cited in the previous chapter:

> LOS ANGELES — In response to the worst drought in California history, Gov. Pete Wilson yesterday named an emergency task force to deal with the critical water shortage and Los Angeles Mayor Tom Bradley called for mandatory water rationing in the city.
>
> The actions came amid discouraging reports of a meager snowpack in the Sierra Nevada and warnings of unprecedented fire danger in Southern California from the prolonged drought and damage caused by an unusually harsh freeze in December.
>
> In Sacramento, Republican Wilson stopped short of declaring a statewide drought emergency but retained the option to do so. He called the drought "a serious threat to California's environment and economy" but said it was not a life-threatening situation that justified pre-empting efforts by local agencies to deal with it.

Here the author waits until the third paragraph before developing either of the two elements in the compound lead to provide readers with meaningful background information.

Whether or not newswriters use a secondary lead, they must prepare the reader for each shift of thought, so that the story appears to flow naturally from topic to topic, and they must include necessary background information without diminishing the reader's interest in the progress of the story. Several techniques that will assist the writer in this task are discussed below.

The fractured paragraph

In composition classes, students learn that the paragraph is the primary unit of composition and that its purpose is to develop a single thought. It contains a topic sentence which expresses that thought and other sentences which expand and elaborate it.

To enhance its topical coherence, the paragraph is given a visual unity. The indentation of each new paragraph cues the reader to the introduction of a new thought. All well and good, but when composition class rules for paragraphing are carried over into newswriting, a problem arises. A typical newspaper column is less than 2¼ inches wide. When an average paragraph of three or four sentences is set in such a narrow space, it becomes a forbidding mass of gray type that severely tests a reader's patience.

Consequently, while attempting to maintain the internal criteria of a good paragraph—unity, order, coherence and completeness—journalists break the visual unity by indenting whenever that will aid readability. They may indent after writing one sentence of a new paragraph if it runs more than three typewritten lines, since an average line of typewritten copy equals approximately two lines of type in a newspaper column. How frequently journalists use this device may be gauged by noting that paragraph length in most American daily newspapers averages less than 1.5 sentences.

To students fresh out of a composition class, newspaper paragraphing seems capricious, but it is not. A closer examination will show that the journalist, while shattering the visual unity of the traditional paragraph, still observes the basic rules for paragraphing—often more scrupulously than other writers who have the built-in unity of the visual paragraph to lean on.

A case in point is the following story from the Associated Press:

WASHINGTON — Governments should cut income taxes and replace the revenues with heavy "green taxes" on polluting fuels, hazardous wastes, pesticides and other environmental threats, the Worldwatch Institute said yesterday.

Such taxes could raise more than $130 billion annually in the United States, allowing at least a 30 percent reduction in income taxes, the environmental research organization said in its annual State of the World report.

The new taxes would "preserve the strengths of a competitive market economy while encouraging individuals and companies to alter their practices in ways that restore the environment," the institute said.

"The challenge we're facing is how to convert an economy which is not environmentally sustainable to one that is," said Lester Brown, Worldwatch president. "The key to doing that, we think, is tax policy."

The most significant of the proposed green taxes would assess $100 per ton for the carbon content of fossil fuels, such as coal, gasoline and natural gas.

A tax at that level would raise consumer energy costs, leading to a drop in consumption that would cut U.S. carbon-dioxide emissions by 20 percent by 2005, helping avert threatened global warming, the report said.

Brown said that the proposed green taxes might fall disproportionately on poor people and that they should be compensated, perhaps, through direct payments.

The report, to be published in 21 languages, includes chapters on urban transportation, abortion, waste reduction, forestry, and Eastern European environmental damage.

Brown said a chapter on the military's worldwide effects on the environment had been written before the Persian Gulf war and dealt only with peacetime conditions.

The report also urges replacing the gross

national product as the chief measure of a country's economic health. The report says the GNP fails to account for environmental factors.

"GNP becomes an obsolete measure of progress in a society striving to meet people's needs as efficiently as possible and with the least damage to the environment," the institute said. "What counts is not growth in output, but the quality of goods produced and services rendered."

At first glance, the story seems to be eleven paragraphs long, but if the writer's indentations are ignored and traditional paragraph rules applied, only four real paragraphs remain.

The lead and the three paragraphs that follow it are really one traditional paragraph describing the "green taxes" proposed by the Worldwatch Institute. The fifth, sixth and seventh paragraphs of the story make up another "thought" paragraph that outlines the most significant part of the proposal.

Paragraphs eight and nine are really one paragraph that describes other parts of the proposal, and ten and eleven amount to one paragraph that gives the institute's view of the GNP as a measure of economic health.

Behind the frequent indentions that break up the long mass of type in the above story, the unmistakable presence of the traditional paragraph form can be seen; only its visual unity has been altered. This, then, is the "fractured paragraph" of newswriting. It is done purely for graphic effect—to enhance readability—but it also serves the purposes of the copy desk by permitting information to be added to or deleted from a story with little or no resetting of type.

Use of this technique places obligations on writers who must maintain an orderly and coherent development of ideas while discarding traditional paragraph structure. They must connect the sentences which develop each thought in such a way that the reader perceives the essential unity, even though the visual form has been broken.

To forge these connections, writers rely on three basic devices: key words, transitional words and phrases, and pronoun references.

KEY WORDS

If in newswriting an indention no longer flags a shift in thought, the writer must provide another signal to the reader that a new topic is about to be introduced. One way to do this is to choose a key word or phrase related to the new topic and place it at the beginning of the sentence.

An effective key word is one that breaks the continuity of the preceding thought but at the same time points back to an earlier statement in the story now being developed.

In paragraph five of the Associated Press story cited above, the reporter, who wishes to shift from a general discussion of the Worldwatch Institute's tax proposal to a specific part of it, writes as follows:

> *The most significant* of the proposed green taxes would assess $100 per ton for the carbon content of fossil fuels, such as coal, gasoline and natural gas.

The three italicized words clearly signal the reader that a new thought paragraph is beginning.

Again, when the writer wants to return to a broader discussion of the Worldwatch document, a key word begins the sentence:

> *The report,* to be published in 21 languages, includes chapters on urban transportation, abortion, waste reduction, forestry and Eastern European environmental damage.

Despite numerous indentions, this story is easy for the reader to follow because the writer has marked each shift of thought with a key word or phrase.

TRANSITIONAL WORDS AND PHRASES

Another device that can assist readers in following the development of a complex story is the use of transitional words and phrases—words or groups of words that explicitly indicate the relationship of one idea to another. Such phrases can be used either to introduce a new topic or to link statements developing a single thought.

Used at the beginning of a sentence, transitions such as "meanwhile," "in a related action," or "on the other hand," indicate a shift of topic. Connectives such as "however," "accordingly," and "as a result" are used to indicate relationships between statements, whether they appear at the beginning or within the sentence.

To return to the above example, the writer's use of a transition at the beginning of the second paragraph introduces an expansion of the lead topic:

> *Such taxes* could raise more than $130 billion annually in the United States, allowing at least a 30 percent reduction in income taxes . . .

In the tenth paragraph, the writer uses the transitional word "also" to signal the start of a new thought paragraph:

> The report *also* urges replacing the gross national product as the chief measure of a country's economic health.

Transitional words and phrases are particularly useful in reporting the meetings of public bodies where many disparate actions must be combined in a single, coherent story. In those instances where the shift of thought is unusually abrupt or where the introduction of a new topic may require background information, a transitional paragraph should be written.

PRONOUN REFERENCES

One of the easiest ways to maintain coherence while breaking the traditional paragraph form is to maintain the subject of the topic sentence in the sentences that develop it and to use pronouns as the linking device.

If, for example, in the course of a story a reporter were to write:

> Mayor Livingston warned that unless drastic cost-cutting procedures were adopted

> in all departments during the coming fiscal
> year, the city would face an "unmanageable"
> financial crisis.

The reporter gains maximum coherence in developing this topic by keeping the mayor as the subject of the sentences that follow and by using a pronoun reference:

> He said he had spoken informally to many
> department heads about budgetary cutbacks
> but without any apparent effect.
> He emphasized, however, that there was no
> reason for panic as long as city officials and
> Council were willing to support his proposals.

By using this device, the essential thought paragraph remains a coherent unit, even though broken into three paragraphs of type. Pronoun references can be used just as effectively with place names, published statements, and collective and other nonpersonal nouns.

Information weaving

No matter what kind of story a reporter writes, he or she must include enough details and background information to make the news fully understandable to the reader. In the case of spot news, getting this kind of information is seldom difficult since the reporter gathers all the necessary data in one place. In other types of stories that involve technical references or a connection to previous events, the reporter may have to make an extra effort to fill in those gaps that would render the story incomplete.

Many beginning journalists fail to provide adequate background information because they are unable to put themselves in the place of the reader. They write, instead, from the privileged position of one fully acquainted with the facts, and the result is a story full of holes that leaves readers puzzled and irritated. Once aware of the problem, however, some beginners run to the opposite extreme: They write paragraphs of solid background information that brings the movement of the story to an abrupt halt. Nothing diminishes reader interest more quickly than a series of such "information blocks."

The ideal solution is to move the necessary details and background information into the story in such a way that the movement never stops. This can be done by placing such material in subordinate clauses while reserving main clauses for the progress of the story—a process called "information weaving." At times the amount of background required for a story makes it difficult to use this technique, but such times will be rare if writers remain aware of their duty to maintain reader interest and construct sentences and paragraphs accordingly.

In this *Washington Post* story about a United Parcel Service driver charged with stealing 850 handguns from his route, the writer effectively weaves in background information (italicized):

> Authorities worked for three years to unravel the gunrunning case, which they say involved the regular theft of UPS packages shipped from Interarms Inc. in Alexandria, *one of the world's largest gun dealerships.*
>
> The guns, *packed in cartons of 20 or more weapons,* were picked up at Interarms and stolen before they reached the UPS distribution center in Alexandria . . .
>
> Officials said the stolen handguns, *which included foreign imports and high-capacity 9 mm semi-automatic pistols,* were stored at an Alexandria home, then taken to Harlem and immediately sold for $200 to $500 each.

If the italicized material in the above example had been put in separate sentences, this might have been the result:

> Authorities worked for three years to unravel the gunrunning case, which they say involved the regular theft of UPS packages shipped from Interarms Inc. in Alexandria. The firm is one of the world's largest gun dealerships.
>
> The guns were picked up at Interarms and stolen before they reached the UPS distribution center in Alexandria. They were packed in cartons of 20 or more weapons.
>
> Officials said the stolen handguns were stored at an Alexandria home, then taken to

> Harlem and immediately sold for $200 to
> $250 each. They included foreign imports and
> high-capacity 9 mm semi-automatic pistols.

In this version, story movement slows down considerably and the writing becomes monotonous. Good writers realize that any sentence used solely to provide background information breaks continuity, so—whenever possible—they try to provide this information within the framework of a sentence that drives the story forward.

Ending the story

If the analogy of the inverted pyramid is carried to its geometric conclusion, the form ultimately narrows down to a point at which it ends. So do most news stories. After dealing with the major facets of the news, the story turns to minor details, and when these have been exhausted, it trails to an end.

This is normal procedure, and with most of the routine news that passes through a newspaper, it is the only feasible one. Yet from time to time, writers will find themselves involved with a news story that, for one reason or another, deserves a deliberate ending. The ending obviously cannot be a comment by the writer, nor can it be a punch line that appears strained or redundant. In some situations, an effective ending might be a particularly striking direct quote that sums up the essence of the story or simply a statement of fact that provides an ironic but accurate perspective on the news. In either case, the writer is justified in using the material for an ending—as long as the overall integrity of the story remains intact.

In a *Los Angeles Times* story about federal regulators' attempts to determine prior to auction whether properties seized from failed savings and loans have environmental value, the writer closes with a quote that sums up the overall thrust of the news:

> Some environmentalists call for restrictions
> on what developers can do with environ-
> mentally sensitive properties. Others want
> properties sold at little or no cost to
> preservation agencies for wildlife sanctuaries
> or parks.

> "We feel very strongly that the federal government has already purchased this property," said Karen Berky, legislative representative in Washington of the Nature Conservancy. "We should do something good with it."

News story endings also can provide an ironic commentary on the news. A *Philadelphia Inquirer* story tells of a visit by Pennsylvania Gov. Robert Casey to Middletown, Pa., to inspect 500 pregnant cows about to be shipped to the Canary Islands by the Pennsylvania Holstein Association under a state-endorsed program called "Operation Cow-Lift." The governor's visit, the story notes, "was intended to stress the importance, particularly for Pennsylvania's agriculture industry, of finding foreign markets for the state's goods."

But the story ends with this paragraph:

> Although the association's deal with the Canary Islands is a symbol of the type of export business the state wants to promote, part of the operation runs counter to another Casey administration goal—bringing more business to the Port of Philadelphia. The cows are being shipped Monday from the Port of Wilmington.

When handling stories of more than routine significance, reporters should check their notes for material that might provide a strong ending.

4 The Elements of News Style

EARLIER CHAPTERS of this book emphasized the role of technology in shaping the language of the newspaper. This phenomenon should not be understood as one peculiar to journalism. Technological force is at work in all historical eras on all kinds of writing, but only in periods of rapid change, such as the 19th century, can its effects be observed more easily.

The invention of movable type in the 15th century radically altered the printing process and, ultimately, the kind of writing that would pass through it. During the next 400 years, the luxuriant writing styles that flourished owed as much to Gutenberg's invention as they did to any author's originality.

Prior to this breakthrough, writing that appeared in book form first had to be carved by hand on page-sized wooden blocks for printing. Given the arduous and time-consuming nature of this process, it is no wonder that few authors—other than those who claimed to be speaking for the Deity—were considered worthy enough for its application.

Movable type broke the bottleneck of the earlier printing

technology and in the process created the "author"—someone who writes for an audience of readers. Looking back at the literature that followed, it seems as if its creators, intoxicated by the power of the new medium, spilled out word upon word in lavish abandon.

That exuberant spirit infected Jonathan Swift, writing more than 200 years after Gutenberg, as he opened his essay on "The Art of Political Lying":

> We are told the Devil is the father of lies, and was a liar from the beginning; so that, beyond contradiction, the invention is old; and, which is more, his first essay of it was purely political, employed in undermining the authority of his prince, and seducing a third part of the subjects from their obedience: for which he was driven down from heaven, where (as Milton expresses it) he had been viceroy of a great western province; and forced to exercise his talent in inferior regions among other fallen spirits, poor or deluded men, whom he still daily tempts to his own sin, and will ever do so, till he be chained in the bottomless pit.

An extreme example, Swift's sentence nevertheless reflects the tendencies of an English prose style that pushed syntax and sentence structure to the utmost limits, piling clause on clause, figure on figure, and withheld the main idea for use as a climactic ending.

This extravagant style persisted well into the 19th century; Charles Dickens, writing in 1859, was not immune, as his often-quoted opening to *A Tale of Two Cities* indicates:

> It was the best of times, it was the worst of times, it was the age of wisdom, it was the age of foolishness, it was the epoch of belief, it was the epoch of incredulity, it was the season of Light, it was the season of Darkness, it was the spring of hope, it was the winter of despair, we had everything before us, we had nothing before us, we were all going direct to heaven, we were all going direct the other way—in short, the period was so far like the present period, that some of its noisiest authorities insisted on its being received, for good or for evil, in the superlative degree of comparison only.

The best writers of this period, like Dickens, gave a vigor and clarity to the style by their deft choice of words and by arranging clauses in such a way that the length of the sentence did not necessarily diminish its coherence. What would ultimately curtail this expansive prose was not a new school of writers but a new environment created by the telegraph press.

Once the electric telegraph became the primary transmitter of news, a new technological bottleneck was placed on the craft of writing. Regardless of their stylistic preferences, journalists who used the telegraph to transmit news were forced to meet its technical demands. Writing style, therefore, is not—as many students suspect— an arbitrary set of rules, but a discipline created by the need to communicate with a reader through a particular medium.

This concept of style does not rule out originality or inventiveness on the writer's part. Even while adhering closely to the discipline of the craft, good writers manage to find their own unique modes of expression. In poetic writing, for instance, the sonnet is one of the most rigorously controlled forms; yet every major poet who used the form—from William Shakespeare to Elizabeth Barrett Browning—left an indelible personal mark upon it.

Newspaper style evolved into its present form during the past 150 years. It has been shaped by the telegraph, the typewriter, the telephone and other 19th-century inventions, and it continues to change in response to the new electronic and cybernetic technology of today.

Contemporary newswriting reflects the journalist's attempt to reach the widest possible audience through the newspaper medium. Its language is direct and vigorous and—for the sake of clarity—favors the simple declarative sentence with just enough variation to avoid monotony. Sentences are built around a noun and verb; all other words and phrases must contribute tellingly to that central relationship. And since journalists try to reach a broad spectrum of readers, they choose short, descriptive and nontechnical words.

In the hands of an expert, modern journalistic style can be forceful, moving and elegant. But even when used by less skillful writers, it usually provides readers with clear and direct access to important information. Whether pros or beginners, newswriters must contend with two important stylistic considerations: word choice and sentence construction.

Choosing the right word

Brevity may be "the soul of wit," as Shakespeare suggested, but ever since the telegraph and the daily newspaper joined forces in newsgathering, it has certainly been an essential component of journalistic writing. Later, when photography became a reporting tool, taking space away from words, and radio and television appeared as alternatives to print, brevity became an overriding consideration.

In the age of electronics, redundancy assumes a double meaning for print journalists. It means that they must avoid not only repeating themselves but also repeating what has been done—and possibly done better—by radio and television. Today's readers, who are also viewers and listeners, have less time for print media. When they turn to print—as they must when seeking information and understanding not available elsewhere—they expect to find it in a concise, interesting form.

Words such as "brief" and "concise" do not necessarily refer to an absolute measurement of length. When applied to newswriting, they mean that the writer should present ideas and information as simply and effectively as possible. This notion of brevity, then, applies to long articles as well as to short ones.

To write in a concise, interesting way, the journalist must begin at the level of words. Each word must justify its place in the sentence or be eliminated. Governing all word choices, however, is the fundamental rule of accuracy, which requires that words evoke in the reader the exact meaning intended by the writer. But writing can be accurate and dull, or accurate and verbose, or—as is often the case—all three.

So for journalists, the choice comes down to this: Among several words, all of which may be accurate, which contributes most to brevity and to the reader's interest and understanding? The best writers will likely choose among four categories of words in making this decision.

SHORT WORDS

Considering the journalistic stress on brevity, newswriters naturally pick the shortest word when given a choice. But the desire for brevity is not the only reason. In English the shortest words are usually the most familiar and, therefore, the most easily understood by a wide range of readers. Still, an even more compelling reason lies behind the use of short words.

Most short English words—such as "home," "friend," "land" and "drunk"—are of Anglo-Saxon origin. These words resonate with greater emotional power than their equivalents of Latin derivation— which in the above case, would be "domicile," "acquaintance," "nation" and "inebriated." In addition to being long, Latin-root words tend to be abstract and emotionally detached in contrast to the strong, vigorous Anglo-Saxon vocabulary.

The following lead from the *Chicago Tribune* shows how short words in a simple structure can generate maximum impact:

> 1992 began in Chicago the same way 1991
> ended, with a hail of gunfire.

Many beginning journalists feel that relying on short, familiar words somehow detracts from the literary quality of their writing. This is simply not true. The best contemporary writers use simple words; the writer's power comes from the images the words create. Only the pretentious writer seeks out longer and more complex words when short ones will do.

Winston Churchill, the great British statesman, was a master of the English language in its spoken and written forms. He wrote a four-volume history of the English-speaking peoples and a six-volume history of World War II, in which he played so critical a role. Yet, many people remembered him best for a speech he gave as prime minister, rallying the British against the Nazis. The most frequently quoted passage in that speech is a sentence containing four short Anglo-Saxon words: "I have nothing to offer but blood, toil, tears and sweat."

CONCRETE WORDS

It has always been true that writing which enables the reader to see, hear or feel the events described communicates more effectively than writing which speaks in abstract or general terms, but this fact takes on added meaning today. Contemporary readers, who receive an increasingly larger share of their information from television, radio, film and photography, have come to expect of the printed word a vividness that at least approaches the sensory power of these newer media.

Aware of the pressure of electronic media on the printed word, some newspapers have gone so far as to hire writing "coaches," who work with reporters to improve the quality of their writing. Coached or not, writers in print media must choose words that evoke a sensory response in the reader.

This lead, from *The Denver Post,* helps the reader to "see" the news:

> Stacey Jo Rose's smile and emerald green dress sparkled last night as she accepted her winning crown at the 1992 Miss Colorado Pageant.

The rule stated in the second chapter that writers should select concrete, specific verbs applies equally to nouns and adjectives. In fact, nouns should be as specific as the context allows. A reporter should not write, "Police found a gun in the victim's overnight bag," when the "gun" is known to be a .38-caliber revolver. Nor should a journalist describe a man as an "outstanding athlete" if he won a silver medal in the Olympic decathlon.

Just how effectively specific references can be used to generate interest in a story can be seen in this lead from a *Des Moines Register* feature by Dirck Steimel:

> Bob Stille never imagined a small patch of shallow water on his northern Iowa farm could lead to a virtual explosion in the diversity of wildlife there. But it has.
>
> Only a few months after he built a small dike that brought a wetland back to life on his Hancock County farm he has seen colorful wood ducks begin nesting in the marshy area, 400 lesser scaup (bluebill ducks) on a layover as they headed north, and a fawn basking in the sunshine on the shoreline. And, just the other night, Stille noticed goldfinches and other songbirds flitting through the marsh at dusk.

> "This is really the greatest thing," Stille, 58, said of 10½ acres of pastureland he converted to a marsh last October. "It's good for water quality, it's good for wildlife and it's really good for people. I get an awful lot of enjoyment and relaxation out of it."

Since nouns and verbs carry the major burden of communication in newswriting, adjectives are used sparingly; as Mark Twain said: "When in doubt, strike it out." Adjectives should only be used to heighten impact—and then be chosen with care and precision.

Weak adjectives like "very" add nothing to the sentence. To describe a woman as "a very good photographer" is the sign of a lazy writer. The skilled journalist might refer to her as a "professional photographer" or an "award-winning photographer."

By using concrete and specific words, writers keep their ideas in sharp focus, enabling the reader to follow the story with a minimum of effort.

NONTECHNICAL WORDS

Every major area of study, from archaeology to zoology, and every profession, trade and technical field has its own distinctive language. As puzzling as they may appear to the uninitiated, these languages serve a real purpose. They permit persons working within a sphere of activity to speak to each other with greater precision, speed and clarity. Much of the formal education required for entering a specialized field consists simply of learning the professional language.

Scientific and technological advances of the 20th century have accentuated the problem that specialized languages pose for journalists. Since they are responsible for informing the public of scientific breakthroughs, journalists must understand the technical language related to the news—yet avoid using it in their stories. This requires that newswriters develop the ability to express technical concepts in short, familiar words and to describe complex processes by using analogies readers understand. When technical words are included—as often they must be—they should be explained immediately in simple language.

The task of translating technical jargon into common language is not restricted to writers who specialize in covering such traditionally confounding areas as science, law, medicine or finance. The challenge may arise in any story, and every competent writer should be able to deal with it.

In a *Boston Globe* nature story on the mosquito, writer Sy Montgomery explains the complex process of a simple mosquito bite:

> The mosquito's proboscis looks like a straw, but actually it's a top and bottom lip, four sets of cutters, and a saliva-injecting syringe, all of it so thin and so long it can be inserted easily into the skin. Then the cutters saw back and forth through the tissue, slicing small blood vessels open. An undisturbed mosquito will thrust and withdraw her mouthparts into the skin five to ten times before locating enough blood for a full meal. Often she will insert the proboscis bent back towards her body, and then she'll have to stand on only her rear legs to feed so the proboscis can straighten out. If you let her feed till full, her abdomen, filled with four times her own weight in blood, will look like a red Christmas tree light, and she'll fly away logey.

In this example, the writer presents technical information so simply and understandably that the reader is unaware of having been given a lesson in entomology—which may be the best criterion for newswriting that attempts to translate information from specialized fields.

The rule about avoiding specialized language in newswriting also applies to nontechnical jargons, such as teen-age slang, Madison Avenue coinages and the inflated speech of bureaucracy, better known to newspaper reporters as "gobbledygook." Journalists who wish to be understood use standard English in its simplest and most vivid forms.

UNSPOILED WORDS

There is no easier way to kill freshness and vigor in writing than to use words and phrases whose imagery has been dulled by repetition. Reliance on trite words and banal figures is the mark of an unimaginative writer, and readers subjected to such writing feel like patrons in a four-star restaurant who find themselves dining on warmed-over food.

Vigorous writing is fresh and immediate. It is produced by writers who choose words with extreme care, building images that fit the ideas they wish to express. Clichés are ready-made images which—even when accurate—give writing a shopworn quality.

So vast is the number of clichés and stale expressions in current usage that even good writers, unless they remain vigilant, are likely to use them. Better to use no figure at all than to say that the damaged freighter "limped into port," that police "combed the neighborhood" looking for suspects or that homeowners made "Herculean efforts" to halt rising floodwaters.

In this lead from an Associated Press story, the writer created a fresh image, and the result is obvious:

> WASHINGTON — Starting next week, GI Joe and Jill will not be just numbers to the Army. They'll also be unique and individual entries in a *frozen library* of blood smears and saliva swabs.

Journalists should avoid straining for substitutes, using words like "launch" and "inaugurate" in place of "begin," and routinely eliminate all trite expressions such as "lingering illness," "general public," "sweeping changes" and "last-ditch effort" whenever they appear.

Writing good sentences

All the guidelines suggested earlier for the construction of an effective lead sentence apply to the writing of good sentences throughout the story. Yet while the lead must be able to stand alone as an independent statement, most sentences in a story serve either to expand and elaborate a previous thought or to shift the story smoothly to a new topic. Their effectiveness is determined more by how well they carry out these objectives than by any virtues they might possess in isolation. Thus, within stories, sentence construction always relates to *context*—that is, the role that the sentence plays in the paragraph.

SENTENCE STYLE

Once past the lead, writers should still try to keep sentence length to a minimum. At the same time they must recognize that *variety* sparks reader interest. Simple and complex declarative sentences are preferred, but periodic forms may be used sparingly for special emphasis.

Word order follows the pattern set in the lead. The beginning of the sentence continues to be the important position, especially in topic sentences where key words are emphasized, but now the writer must also take into account the need for continuity and smooth transitions.

Active voice remains the essential mode of sentence construction. Writers should take care not to slip into unemphatic passive voice and inactive verb forms.

Selecting strong verbs continues as a fundamental requirement for an effective sentence, but within a story the range of verb choices may narrow considerably from those available in lead writing. As the writer moves from lead to elaboration, accurate verbs tend to be less vivid, and in attributing quoted matter, "said" will be the most often used verb.

Throughout the story, proper subordination of minor sentence elements provides the key to clarity and understanding. Skillful use of this technique, as noted in the earlier section on information weaving, permits several ideas to be combined in a sentence but in such a way that the relationship to the main idea is always clear to the reader. The alternative would be a monotonous succession of short sentences in which each idea is equally emphasized and unrelated to others.

In good newswriting, every sentence moves the story forward. A sentence that does not is a wasted sentence and probably was built on background information or on a minor element that belongs in a subordinate clause.

SENTENCE CRITERIA

The writer's goal is to produce not the perfect sentence but a pattern of sentences that is cohesive, clear and interesting.

Cohesion ultimately is the product of strong organization, but the skillful use of connectives and transitional devices can heighten it. Clarity is obtained by keeping sentence elements properly related to each other through subordination and coordination, by checking the agreement of nouns and verbs, and by making sure pronoun references are accurate.

Interesting copy—the hallmark of the professional writer—begins with a constant awareness of the readers and their preferences. It overcomes reader inertia by the sheer force of inventiveness and, at the level of the sentence, is expressed by variety both in sentence length and structure.

Most errors in sentence writing are sins against clarity. They can be grouped into two broad categories: problems caused by failing to clarify the relationship of ideas that belong together and those caused by connecting ideas that do not belong together.

FAULTY RELATIONSHIPS

The sentence error committed most frequently—even by working journalists—is the *dangling modifier.* This term describes a verbal phrase, usually at the beginning of a sentence, that "dangles" because the subject it should modify is either missing from the sentence or not easily discernible. As a result, the meaning of the sentence blurs, as in these examples:

> To qualify for the new supervisory positions in the sanitation department, an examination must be passed.

> Having argued against the proposed ordinance, the hearing was recessed and the mayor left with her aides.

In the first example, the subject of the opening phrase is missing from the sentence. When it is inserted, the sentence reads:

> To qualify for the new supervisory positions in the sanitation department, applicants must pass an examination.

In the second example, the intended subject is within the sentence but disconnected from the modifier. To make this relationship clear, the sentence should read:

> Having argued against the proposed ordinance, the mayor left with her aides when the hearing was recessed.

Whenever a verbal phrase is used to open a sentence, the writer should make sure that the subject modified immediately follows the comma setting off that phrase.

Less common than the dangling modifier but no less confusing is the *squinting modifier,* a phrase or clause that because of its position in the sentence can be read as modifying either of two words:

> The senator returned to the town where he was born in 1927 in a limousine.

It is unlikely that the senator was born in a limousine. The writer should have eliminated the confusion by restructuring the sentence:

> Riding in a limousine, the senator returned to the town where he was born in 1927.

Another common error in sentence construction arises from the failure to observe the fundamental rule of *parallelism,* which requires that parallel elements in a sentence be expressed in parallel form.

In this sentence, the parallel elements are not expressed in parallel form:

> The newly established Human Relations Commission has the power to investigate complaints, hold hearings, of subpoenaing witnesses and penalizing violators of the city's fair housing code.

The effect of shifting forms jars the reader. For clarity, the four elements require parallel structure, as follows:

> The newly established Human Relations Commission has the power to investigate

> complaints, hold hearings, subpoena
> witnesses and penalize violators of the city's
> fair housing code.

Many journalists who are normally conscientious about observing parallel form err when using the "either-or" or "not only-but" constructions. They write:

> To require that each store owner submit
> proposed external signs and decorations to
> the art commission for approval would not
> only be unworkable but uneconomic,
> witnesses testified.

To be clear, this construction requires that the element following "not only" be grammatically parallel to the element following "but." In the above example, "not only" is followed by a verb and "but" by an adjective. A simple transposition restores parallel form:

> To require that each store owner submit
> proposed external signs and decorations to
> the art commission for approval would be not
> only unworkable but uneconomic, witnesses
> testified.

Everyone learns at some point about the *agreement of pronouns and antecedents,* yet the frequent use of the pronouns "they" and "their" in news stories to refer to nouns such as "council," "board," "company" and "team" suggests that many journalists are unaware that these are singular nouns and require the singular pronouns "it" or "its."

Use of the pronoun "it" can also create problems if the sentence contains more than one antecedent to which the "it" might refer. For example:

> Council voted to hold the planning
> commission fully responsible for its decisions.

In this case, ambiguity can be eliminated by making one of the nouns plural:

> Council members voted to hold the
> planning commission fully responsible for its
> decisions.

Writers who seek clarity must avoid all unnecessary changes of perspective within the sentence, especially *shifts of subject and voice*. A shift of one may also cause a shift of the other.

It is awkward to say:

> The governor spent a working vacation at
> Aspen, Colo., and all of his free time was
> devoted to skiing.

This sentence can be improved simply by maintaining a single subject:

> The governor spent a working vacation at
> Aspen, Colo., and devoted all of his free time
> to skiing.

Writers also should stay alert to shifts in the voice of verbs within a sentence:

> Senator Simon sought his party's
> nomination for president in 1988 but was
> defeated by Michael Dukakis.

Vigor is retained by keeping all verbs in the active voice:

> Senator Simon sought his party's
> nomination for president in 1988 but lost to
> Michael Dukakis.

Another problem for writers is the sequence of verb forms in a sentence, commonly referred to as *sequence of tenses*. The general rule states that all verbs in a sentence should be related to the tense of the main clause, which in newswriting is normally the past tense.

Yet sentences like these pop up with amazing frequency in even the best newspapers.

> He said he is concerned about the un-
> employment rate.

> He testified that he wrote the letter because
> he was angry at the kind of treatment he had
> received.

The specific rule violated here requires verbs in subordinate clauses to take the tense of the verb in the main clause. Thus, the first sentence should be written:

> He said he was concerned about the
> unemployment rate.

Why, then, is the second example incorrect? Because the rule further states that verbs in subordinate clauses that relate to events prior in time to the governing verb must be moved one stage further back in the past.

Consequently, the second example should take this form:

> He testified that he had written the letter
> because he had been angry at the kind of
> treatment he had received.

It should be noted that the last verb in the sequence, "had received," was originally in the past perfect tense. Since there is no tense more remote than past perfect, the verb remains unchanged.

The following construction often appears in newswriting:

> He wrote the letter, he testified, because he
> was angry at the kind of treatment he had
> received.

This sentence is correct because "he testified" is a parenthetical clause, not the governing verb of the sentence.

There is one exception to the sequence-of-tenses rule and it occurs when the statement made in the subordinate clause is permanently true. Thus, a journalist could correctly write:

> She said that the diameter of the moon is
> 2,160 miles.

Reporting truisms, however, is seldom a concern for journalists.

FALSE RELATIONSHIPS

If a sentence should express a single thought, then all its parts must relate in some way to a central idea. When they do not, sentence unity is destroyed and the reader is confused. In their singleminded concern for brevity, many beginning writers force together unrelated material and produce sentences like this:

> Born in Des Moines, he was an active trial lawyer, specializing in workmen's compensation cases.

Readers expect to find a connection between these two ideas. When they cannot, they are annoyed and begin to lose interest in the story. While a subject's place of birth rarely merits a sentence of its own, it should be subordinated in a sentence where a natural relationship can be made, such as in this one:

> Born in Des Moines, he attended public schools in that city and graduated in 1926 from the State University of Iowa.

The problem also can arise with parenthetical phrases, which, as every writer soon learns, make excellent hiding places for necessary details. But in sentences like the following one, the device should not be used:

> Miller, 45, a systems analyst for the Social Security Administration, struck the fleeing suspect on the head with his briefcase.

Here, irrelevant material juxtaposed in a narrative sentence stops the action and spoils the flow of the story.

Both of the above examples are fairly obvious violations of sentence unity. A less obvious but even more common problem is the combining of ideas that seem to be related, yet not closely enough for the reader to see the connection. The problem occurs most often when reporters, working against a deadline, try to wrap up a report on a meeting or a press conference that includes many disparate topics. They will be tempted to write something like this:

Councilman Cohen urged residents who support the proposed zoning ordinance to make known their feelings at the April hearing and announced that sealed bids on sewer construction would be opened at the next council meeting.

Separate ideas belong in separate sentences. Any time saved by the writer in combining them is lost by the reader in trying to figure out the relationship.

5 The Spoken Word in Print

EVER SINCE the 1880s, when the telephone entered the newsroom to become a tool of modern journalism, the availability of the direct quote has made it an integral part of newswriting.

A reporter with a telephone at his or her elbow gains immediate access to persons involved in the news as well as to those likely to be affected by it. Thus, in every significant news story, editors look first for direct quotes from the principals. If they are not to be found, writers will need an exceptionally convincing answer for the inevitable question from the copy desk.

Why are direct quotes such a desirable feature of the contemporary news story? The most compelling reason is that they offer readers the maximum degree of personal contact with newsmakers obtainable in print. If in most writing journalists function as intermediaries between the reader and the event, by using direct quotes they can at least step aside and let their subjects speak for themselves.

Direct quotes are especially important in stories that hinge on controversial or inflammatory statements. By providing a full quote of the statement in question, writers protect themselves from the charge that their leads inaccurately interpret the speaker's words. Accuracy aside, direct quotes also give the reader a more intimate glimpse of the subject's style and character. For this reason they are an essential ingredient—in many instances, the dominant one—of the personality feature.

Liberal use of direct quotes enables writers to inject a considerable degree of variety into stories. Any story that is limited to a paraphrasing of the subject's remarks quickly becomes monotonous and dull. In the hands of a skillful writer, however, the interplay between paraphrase and direct quote gives stories a vitality unmatched in other forms of journalistic writing.

One of the more significant effects of electronic media on print journalism during the past several decades has been the increased pressure on print journalists to approximate the immediacy of radio and television. Radio re-emphasized the spoken word and the power of the human voice; television, with its unique ability to scan the features and mannerisms of its subjects, added a whole new dimension to personal reporting. As a result, journalists who wish to hold the attention of contemporary readers must flavor their writing with the personal vividness that only direct quotes and dialogue can provide.

To quote or not to quote

The first task facing reporters in handling a subject's remarks is to decide at the outset which should be used and which should be ignored. Newsworthiness, of course, is the basic criterion, but this standard tends to be applied in different ways in different situations.

In the case of speeches, which will be examined in greater detail in the next chapter, the news criteria must be applied rigorously if a 30-minute speech is to be reported in a half column of type. In a rare interview with a prominent figure, however, news emphasis is relaxed somewhat so that the reader can obtain a more coherent picture of the subject's views.

Once these underlying considerations have been taken into account and a decision made as to what comments will be used, the writer must still decide when to quote and when to paraphrase.

DIRECT QUOTES

As previously noted, all controversial material should be presented in direct quotes, along with any preceding or following remarks required for context. Similarly, in court reporting, all statements by principals relating to crucial points in a trial should be given in direct quotes. In a *Boston Globe* story about a judge's decision to try a 17-year-old youth for murder as an adult, the writer explains the ruling by quoting Salem District Court Judge Brian Merrick:

> "No alcohol, drug or goading taunt caused Fuller to commit this murder," Merrick said, rejecting defense claims that Fuller's actions were driven by his abuse of alcohol and steroids and a history of depression. "Fuller's conduct in relation to Amy had been jealous, possessive, controlling, violent and blaming."

In other kinds of stories, where controversy does not factor in, the writer uses direct quotes for remarks that express the subject's views in a particularly striking or emphatic manner. The following direct quote comes from a story in the *Philadelphia Inquirer* about the arrest in Wilmington, Del., of 28 young professionals on charges of cocaine possession, delivery and trafficking:

> "Many of them were . . . born with a golden spoon in their mouths, and I guess they decided to put it up their noses," Capt. Ronald Huston of the Wilmington vice squad said of those arrested.

This direct quote is a pungent comment on the news by a police official. Any attempt to paraphrase it would destroy its emphatic quality.

Even when a writer does not build a story around the statements of subjects in the news, a well-chosen direct quote can heighten impact by revealing in a flash the feelings or emotional states of participants. In this Associated Press story, a direct quote in the second paragraph catches a father's reaction to his son's predicament:

> ERIE, Pa. — A 3-year-old boy took the tiller of his family's catamaran on Lake Erie on Sunday and sailed two miles to shore by himself, leaving his father, brother and two cousins in the water.
>
> "I wondered where he was going," said the father, Tom Craut, 33, as his son, Andy, sailed away. "Then I thought, 'Dang, he's going all the way to the beach!'"
>
> A passing boat picked up the floating foursome . . .

In another AP account of a near disaster, a second-paragraph quote describes the effect on a city:

> DULUTH, Minn. — A cloud of toxic vapor from a derailed tank car forced at least 50,000 people to flee homes and businesses Tuesday in Minnesota and Wisconsin, creating traffic jams and leaving downtown Duluth deserted.
>
> "It's an absolute ghost town. It's eerie what's going on down there," Mayor Gary Doty said at an emergency command post outside the city.
>
> At least 25 people were taken to hospitals in the two states, and about 260 National Guard and Army Reserve troops mobilized . . .

Thus, as a general rule, direct quotes should be used for revelatory comments—comments that explain or crystallize a subject's views in a telling manner. Quotation marks accentuate whatever they enclose, and a direct quote ought to justify that emphasis. Commonplace remarks or comments that are obvious, repetitious or incoherent should not be quoted.

PARAPHRASE

When it becomes necessary to include comments by a subject that are not expressed clearly or emphatically—and most colloquial speech is not—the writer turns to the paraphrase. By using this device, writers can restructure or condense the material in a way that will hold the reader's interest.

In stories based on interviews, speeches or courtroom testimony, the paraphrase also serves an important transitional function. It enables the writer to change the topic or the speaker smoothly and set the stage for the next direct quote. Paraphrases (italicized) are used for both purposes in this excerpt from a Reuters story on the refusal of several retail chains to stock an AIDS prevention book by basketball star Earvin "Magic" Johnson:

> Spokesmen for Wal-Mart and Kmart did not return phone calls, but a Wal-Mart spokesman was quoted by the Detroit News as saying, "The language was not in keeping with what our customers tell us they would want to read."
>
> *The stores are well within their rights to keep the AIDS book off their shelves,* said retail consultant Alan Millstein.
>
> "There is no reason that I can think of to force a retailer to sell anything that he doesn't want to sell or doesn't think there is a market for," Millstein said.
>
> *Besides, Johnson's book may not be any good,* Millstein said: "Magic Johnson may score high when it comes to baskets and free throws, but in the literary world he's an unknown quantity and most celebrity books flop anyway."

By skillfully using the paraphrase, writers maintain control over their material. They can sum up rambling, obtuse statements in a single sentence; they can combine related ideas that are separated in the subject's own words; and they can shift the story deftly from topic to topic and from speaker to speaker.

Even greater variety may be obtained in paraphrasing by occasionally using the *indirect quotation.* This form of the paraphrase resembles the direct quote in style, with attribution inserted in a parenthetical clause. It usually appears this way:

> The present tuition rate can only be maintained, he said, by increased subsidies from the state legislature.

Indirect quotations permit the writer to come as close as possible to the speaker's syntax while still allowing for condensation and for the correction of awkward sentence structure. Indirect quotes also enable the writer to keep the speaker's remarks in their original tense.

Well-written stories based on quoted material display a subtle alternation between paraphrase and direct quote—a kind of ebb and flow—that in no small measure accounts for their unique interest and texture.

ACCURACY

When using direct quotes, writers must make sure they are as accurate as possible. This means that the words attributed to the speaker must be the words the speaker used, with the exception of articles—"a" in place of "the" and vice versa—and an occasional minor word. Since accuracy in the handling of quotes directly relates to accuracy in reporting, some tips on covering speeches and press conferences have been included in the next chapter.

In paraphrasing a subject's remarks, writers still must meet a high standard of accuracy. Paraphrased statements should reflect substantially what the subject said, although expressed in the writer's words. Since paraphrasing consists in converting the actual words of the subject into a more "generic" form, it should not be used for striking comments that would be more effective as direct quotes. Writers should also avoid using colorful or overly specific words in paraphrasing, as readers may conclude that those are the subject's words.

Since there are no punctuation marks in colloquial speech—despite comedian Victor Borge's hilarious attempt to create them—one of the writer's tasks in dealing with direct quotes is to punctuate them correctly. This means rendering the speaker's comments into complete sentences of standard English with commas, periods, dashes and question marks inserted where appropriate. Consequently, writers must clearly understand punctuation rules before they set out to impose them on the speech of others.

When speakers leave out key words in a sentence or use pronouns whose antecedents may be unclear to the reader, the writer who wishes to use the statement as a direct quote must insert the missing information in brackets or parentheses. Since these punctuation marks diminish the impact of direct quotes, writers should use them infrequently. Comments requiring extensive reconstruction should be paraphrased rather than quoted.

A question related to accuracy arises when the writer confronts ungrammatical quotes: Should they be corrected? The strongest argument for correction is based on an awareness that grammatical errors common to colloquial speech seem more grievous when transferred to print. Most writers routinely correct these errors if they feel the speaker would have eliminated them in writing. But when a subject's overall speech pattern is marked by an absence of grammar, to correct the errors would create a false impression of the speaker.

The mechanics of quoting

For many beginners, the most difficult part of handling direct quotes is mastering the stylistic requirements necessary for proper attribution. If, at first, the rules appear to be somewhat complex and arbitrary, they will take on greater meaning as the writer becomes aware of their objective: to leave no doubt in the reader's mind about who is speaking.

The fundamental rule of attribution, therefore, is that all statements which are not those of the writer clearly connect to the speaker. While this may seem a fairly obvious requirement, many beginning writers experience considerable difficulty in determining what constitutes adequate linkage. Much of this confusion passes once they become aware that the physical paragraph is as important a factor in determining proper attribution as is the sentence. So before moving on, a few comments are in order on the paragraphing of direct quotes.

In Chapter 3 it was explained that newswriting practice breaks the traditional topic paragraph into smaller paragraphs to improve its readability in a newspaper column. When handling direct quotes, journalists find an additional reason for paragraphing: Every new direct quote should be given a new paragraph. This means that in moving from a paraphrase of the speaker's remarks to a direct quote, the writer begins a new paragraph, as in the following example:

Commissioner Rodriguez predicted that an
extensive police investigation of the case was

> about ready to produce results.
> "We have several promising leads and expect to make arrests in the next few days," he said.

Note that the preferred form for attribution in newswriting is "he said" or "she said" or "Rodriguez said" rather than "said Rodriguez." This "attribution tag," as it is called, should appear at the end of the sentence or at a natural break in the sentence—as a general rule—but not at the beginning. Starting the direct quote with attribution makes the quote less emphatic. Note also that quotation marks are placed on the *outside* of commas and periods.

If in the above example the writer continued to quote Commissioner Rodriguez, a new paragraph would not be needed. The quote could read as follows:

> "We have several promising leads and expect to make arrests in the next few days," he said. "We have also received extraordinary cooperation from the business firms who were victimized by this ring."

Once a direct quote has been indented, the only further paragraphing considerations relate to readability. Journalists should indent a long direct quote every two or three sentences.

In presenting direct quotes, writers also use the paragraph to indicate a change of speaker, but rarely does a simple indentation serve as a strong enough signal to the reader that such a shift has taken place. A new speaker is more effectively introduced by a paraphrase in which the speaker's name appears at the beginning as the subject of the sentence:

> Thomas Rogers, a landscape architect who appeared as a witness for the residents, testified that the proposed construction would have a detrimental effect on nearby properties.
> "This project," he said, "will alter the prevailing drainage patterns and more than likely cause serious erosion of adjacent land."

Transitional paragraphs of this kind are essential for clarity, especially in stories where the writer quotes two or more persons.

ATTRIBUTION

Attribution, as noted earlier, simply means insuring that direct quotes are properly linked to the speaker.

In more specific terms, it means that every direct quote must be attributed to someone, and that attribution must appear within the first sentence of the quote. It may be placed at the end of the sentence (as in the first of the two previous examples) or it may be inserted within the sentence (as in the second), but it must appear in the *first sentence.*

Fair enough, but the reader may wonder how far this first-sentence attribution can be extended. If a direct quote has been attributed in the first sentence, the quote can be continued *in the same paragraph* without further attribution, as in this previous example:

> "We have several promising leads and expect to make arrests in the next few days," he said. "We have also received extraordinary cooperation from the business firms who were victimized by this ring."

If the writer uses a long direct quote of two or more paragraphs, the first-sentence attribution can be extended indefinitely as long as one important condition is met: The paragraph containing the attribution must end with quoted material.

Thus, the direct quotes in the above example can be extended simply by removing the quotation marks from the end of the first paragraph—a signal to the reader that the quote will continue—and by placing quotation marks at the beginning of the next paragraph, as follows:

> "We have several promising leads and expect to make arrests in the next few days," he said. "We have also received extraordinary cooperation from the business firms who were victimized by this ring.
>
> "In my ten years as police commissioner, I can't recall an investigation that elicited a comparable degree of community support."

If, on the other hand, the first paragraph of direct quotes should end with attribution, an extension of the direct quote calls for new attribution in the first sentence of the next paragraph, as in this example:

> "We have studied comparable tax programs in six other cities and our most conservative estimate is that this plan will eliminate the operating deficit in three years," the mayor said.
>
> "We have tried to put together a tax program that would be equitable to wage earners, property owners and lower income groups," she said. "I think we have succeeded."

To put it simply, paragraph structure is the key to determining proper attribution. Recognizing this fact, writers who wish to avoid repeating "he said," "she said" or their equivalents in a long direct quote, construct the first paragraph so that attribution does not appear at the end. One way to do this is by inserting attribution at an appropriate break in the sentence. Another method is to conclude the paragraph with a short quoted sentence, as in the second paragraph of the previous example.

Once a running quote has been interrupted by a paraphrase, the directly quoted material that follows the paraphrase is subject to the same rules as the first quote; that is, it must be attributed to the speaker in the first sentence and the attribution extended according to the paragraph rule.

After presenting the second or third direct quote by the same speaker, some writers ignore the rules and present direct quotes without attribution, assuming that the reader will make the connection. This is lazy writing. Variety results from a conscious structuring of paragraphs to eliminate the need for attribution, not simply by omitting it where it is required.

PARTIAL QUOTES

Up to this point, discussion has been limited to *full direct quotes,* meaning direct quotes that are complete sentences. At times in the course of a story writers may wish to quote only words or phrases by the speaker in a sentence of their own. These *partial quotes* should be used sparingly and only for key words or phrases that the writer does not wish to quote in full but feels are important to the story. Their overuse by inexperienced writers shreds quoted matter into meaningless fragments and lessens the impact of direct quotes.

Partial quotes follow the attribution rules for the paraphrase rather than for the full direct quote. Here is an example:

> Councilman Greene described the mayor's tax proposal as "anachronistic" and said it was unlikely to produce "the exaggerated revenues projected by its designers."

Like the paraphrase, a partial quote is normally attributed at the beginning of the sentence. Even when a partial quote ends with quoted material, as does the above example, it should not be extended in this manner:

> Councilman Greene described the mayor's tax proposal as "anachronistic" and said it was unlikely to produce "the exaggerated revenues projected by its designers. There are just too many 'ifs' in the proposal."

Instead, the writer should treat the partial quote as a paraphrase and begin the continuation as a fresh quote with proper attribution, as follows:

> Councilman Greene described the mayor's tax proposal as "anachronistic" and said it was unlikely to produce "the exaggerated revenues projected by its designers."
>
> "There are just too many 'ifs' in the proposal," he added.

These are the essential rules for proper attribution. Their purpose, as noted earlier, is to enable the reader to identify the source of each quote. When they are not followed carefully, confusion results, as shown in the following example from a community newspaper:

> Like Albert Camus, the humanist French writer-philosopher, Father Berrigan is "looking for a world in which murder will no longer be legitimate. It's too much to expect that murder won't occur at all," explained Arthur B. Jellis, the Unitarian Society's minister, introducing the Jesuit priest on March 7.
>
> "Religion often becomes a resource for the same old death game." Father Berrigan urges us to "threaten old stereotypes with new questions, shocking and uncomfortable. At times, one must be unpopular with all sides," Dr. Jellis noted.

This excerpt breaks almost every rule of attribution. In the first paragraph, the reader's confusion about the origin of the direct quote is compounded at the end when a new speaker is introduced. At this point the reader doesn't know whether the quote is from Albert Camus, Father Berrigan or Arthur Jellis. The second paragraph opens with an unattributed quote and concludes with a quote that could be attributed to two possible authors.

Even readers who enjoy puzzles will be frustrated when forced to decipher a news story. By observing the rules of attribution, a writer eliminates this kind of needless confusion.

SUBSTITUTES FOR "SAID"

Writers should make a habit of seeking alternatives to the verb "said," but not at the expense of accuracy or simplicity. Verbs such as "pointed out," "warned," "argued" or "predicted" are good substitutes for "said" because they add meaning to the sentence, but they must accurately reflect the context of the remark.

Here the attempt to find a substitute for "said" produces an incongruous attribution:

> "Now that the election is over, I'm going fishing," the mayor stated.

"Stated" or "declared" tend to be pompous synonyms for "said" and usually are less effective than a repetition of the latter verb. Unless a substitute for "said" actually improves the sentence, writers should stick to using the past tense of "say"—which is what most speakers do most of the time.

Verbs such as "smiled" or "shrugged," which refer to actions rather than to speech, should never be used in place of "said." If the writer wishes to indicate an action related to a comment, the action verb should be combined with attribution in this way:

> "Will I run again—who knows?" he said
> with a shrug.

When writers strain too hard to avoid the use of "said," their efforts become obvious to the reader. That defeats the whole purpose of using direct quotes, which is to put the emphasis on the speaker, not the writer.

6 Varieties of the Basic Structure

FOR MOST of the routine stories that a reporter writes, the inverted pyramid structure outlined in Chapter 3 serves as a useful organizing tool. It works well because a major portion of the events covered by newspapers have as their news focus a single action or element of interest.

Still, the inverted pyramid has its limitations. When the focus of a news story extends beyond a single event in a narrow time frame to encompass a series of actions over a longer period, a different kind of structure is required. Instead of writing a lead with a "today" or "yesterday" peg, the reporter must approach the material from the wider perspective of meaning or significance. These stories generally take the form of the feature and will be discussed in later chapters.

Even within the broad category of what is generally referred to as "straight news," the inverted pyramid model must occasionally be altered to meet the needs of the story. Such alteration is necessary in multielement stories that feature two or more aspects of equal importance. It is also required in stories where a chronology is an essential part of the news interest and in certain specialized news stories such as accounts of public meetings and obituaries.

Thus, while the inverted pyramid is—strictly speaking—a model for one kind of news story, in a broader sense it offers an approach to news that permits writers to cope with a variety of news situations under deadline conditions.

The multielement story

In Chapter 2 it was noted that when two or more aspects of the news were important enough to be emphasized in the lead, the structure of the lead took the form of a compound sentence with coordinating conjunctions linking the key elements. While this shift from complex to compound lead sentence solves the problem of news emphasis in such stories, it creates a dilemma for the writer in developing the lead.

Since both elements of the lead assume equal importance, how does the writer choose which one to develop first? And having chosen one, the writer faces another problem: How long can the reader be kept waiting to learn something about the other element that the writer claims is equally important?

The solution to this problem is a kind of journalistic compromise in which the writer develops both elements alternatively. Take this lead as an example:

> City Council voted last night to expand and overhaul Dover's recreational facilities at a cost of $10.5 million and approved a new amusement tax package to provide funds for the project.

This lead contains two important elements of news for Dover residents: a major capital program coupled with a tax increase. Where to begin? Since the writer put the project first, that is a logical place to start:

> In a 6-3 vote, council adopted a comprehensive plan to bring the city's recreational services up to the level of current demand.

> The plan, based on two separate studies of recreational needs, calls for the construction of two new recreation centers and for renovations to all eight existing centers.

With the major aspects of the project filled in, the writer can turn to the key points of the tax package:

> The tax package, adopted by the same margin, calls for a 2 percent increase in the city amusement tax to 5 percent and the extension of the tax to three categories of amusements formerly exempted from the tax, among them video rentals.
>
> Proponents of the tax measure predicted that it would raise revenues necessary for the recreational improvements within three years.

Now the writer is free to go back and describe the recreation project in detail:

> New recreation centers will be constructed at Main and Jefferson streets on land already owned by the city and at Elmwood Park.
>
> Both centers will include permanent structures with facilities for basketball and gymnastics as well as athletic fields with baseball diamonds and tennis courts.
>
> Renovations to existing centers will include . . .

Once the writer wraps that up, the specifics of the tax package can be provided:

> The new amusement taxes will be levied on video rentals; pay-to-play miniature golf, billiards and table tennis; and children's entertainment conducted for profit.
>
> Owners of video rental stores in the city bitterly opposed the new taxes at several council meetings during the past three months.
>
> Revenues from the new taxes are estimated to produce . . .

In some stories where the news elements are more complex, partial development may continue for another block or two before final elaboration begins. By following this pattern of alternating development, the writer maintains the dual emphasis of the lead through a major portion of the story.

The "hourglass" structure

In learning to write the inverted pyramid story, beginners are constantly warned to avoid slipping into chronology when they should be following order of importance. These admonitions are so frequent that many inexperienced writers may get the idea that there is something inherently wrong with the oldest and most universal method of telling a story.

The inverted pyramid structure, as discussed earlier, evolved out of the journalist's need to get stories through the medium of the telegraph. While the telegraph has long since disappeared as a medium of journalistic communication, the inverted pyramid remains because it serves other purposes just as well. It enables reporters to write news quickly under deadline conditions, it offers copy desks the freedom to cut stories easily as news values change, and it allows readers to judge early in the story whether they wish to continue reading.

Yet there are news stories—even spot news stories—where chronology constitutes an essential part of the account. Stories of crimes, accidents and disasters fall into this category, as do reports of major trials and legal proceedings. To make them fully understandable to the reader, the writer must at some point include a block of narrative that puts events into a time sequence.

Rather than cramp this narrative within the inverted pyramid structure, some writers advocate giving it a featured place of its own at the end. This story form is called the "hourglass" or "double pyramid" because at the point the inverted pyramid ends, the narrative pyramid begins. In this example from the Associated Press, the narrative pyramid begins in paragraph seven:

> PORTLAND, Maine — A crowd of bar patrons watched as a man was beaten,

rammed face-first through a store window and then left to bleed to death on the sidewalk by three assailants, police said yesterday.

No one in the crowd of 35 to 40 people tried to stop the three attackers as they walked away while their victim, Randal B. Toler, 26, lay in a pool of blood late Wednesday night across the street from DeNan's, a downtown bar, police said.

Police arrested Michael Allen Tuck, 29, of Portland, early yesterday morning and charged him with murder. They were searching for the two other men who allegedly attacked Toler.

Tuck pleaded innocent at his arraignment yesterday afternoon and was ordered held without bail in Cumberland County Jail.

Toler, whose last known address was in Holly Hill, Fla., was pronounced dead at Maine Medical Center in Portland at 12:04 a.m. yesterday, less than an hour after the assault.

Dr. Kristin Sweeney, the state's deputy chief medical examiner, said an autopsy showed Toler bled to death from a deep cut to his left armpit that severed a major artery and vein.

Toler and another man were in DeNan's on Free Street when they got into an argument with some other patrons, police said.

Deputy Police Chief Steven Roberts said investigators have received conflicting stories from witnesses about what started the argument. But he confirmed that some witnesses said Toler had urinated on the street outside the bar and apparently had sprayed a woman patron, who went back inside and complained to others.

Toler and his friend, whom police have refused to identify, then were jumped across the street from DeNan's by three men who also had been drinking in the bar, Roberts said.

The friend was immediately knocked unconscious, he said.

"It then became three on one," Roberts said.

In stories containing strong narrative material, the hourglass structure is an effective way of using the age-old power of the story to enhance the news. Its one drawback is that it cannot be cut from the bottom, and indiscriminate use of the form would create problems for copy editors.

The speech story

Stories based on speeches, news interviews and press conferences present a real challenge to the beginning journalist since they demand a clear understanding of relative news values and story structure along with the skillful handling of quoted matter.

One of the hardest things for a beginner to grasp is that the journalist—not the speaker—is the ultimate judge of what is newsworthy. An inexperienced reporter sent out to cover a speech by a prominent public official will likely be overawed by the subject, and, if not careful, will accept the speaker's order of importance.

The reporter must understand that he or she should cover the event as a representative of the newspaper's readers and that the speaker's comments must be judged on the basis of their relevance to this group rather than the speaker's audience, which already has expressed a special interest by attending. This means that reporters may freely disregard the speaker's order altogether and use material they believe will interest the reader in a way that reflects its relative importance.

There are times when remarks made by a speaker during a question-and-answer period following a speech prove more newsworthy than anything said in the prepared address. Occasionally, audience response may be the most significant aspect of the speech. In either case, reporters should have no qualms about building their leads on this material.

The reporter's purpose in covering a speech, as in any other event, is to look for news; it is not to produce a summary of the speaker's remarks. Political candidates may give the same speech over and over during the course of a campaign, but reporters who continue to write stories based on these remarks insult the intelligence of their readers. By refusing to pass on repetitious, irrelevant or frivolous comments by candidates, reporters can help raise the level of political discourse. If the press applied such standards as a general rule, candidates would learn quickly that to get airtime or newspaper space, they must address issues with intelligence and imagination.

In most speech reporting, however, the writer does not need to maintain as rigorous a criteria for newsworthiness. Reporters often cover speeches that are not expected to produce any significant news. Here, factors other than the speech itself may affect news values, such as the appearance of a prominent national figure in the newspaper's area or retirement ceremonies for a well-known public official.

Even in such cases, reporters should keep watch for the most interesting or unusual remarks or audience response that might give their stories a touch of color. A reporter is never released from the obligation to look for news—not even when the odds are against finding it.

THE ADVANCE TEXT

The effort involved in writing the speech story has been lessened somewhat by the almost universal practice of speakers providing the press with an advance copy of their remarks. Writers who have a neatly printed copy of a speech next to their keyboards can prepare a story with a minimum of time and effort. They can quickly leaf through the pages with a red pencil in hand, marking newsworthy or striking passages. By the time they have scanned the whole text, a lead is likely to suggest itself, and they can then build their story with direct quotes that leave no nagging doubts about accuracy.

Writers must also recognize the limitations of the advance text. A printed speech gives no indication of the oral or gestural emphasis that a speaker may add to certain remarks. Nor does it guarantee what the speaker ultimately will say. Encouraged by a responsive audience, speakers may make extemporaneous comments far more newsworthy than anything contained in the prepared text. Thus, if the speech is an important one by a prominent figure, writers should attend even though they may have an advance text. They can then follow the prepared remarks as the subject speaks, noting any changes or additions.

Newspapers with deadlines before the time of the speech can write their stories based on the advance text, but they should protect themselves by including the phrase "in a speech prepared for delivery at 8 p.m. tonight." This lets the reader know that the reporter wrote the story prior to the actual delivery of the address.

NOTE TAKING

Despite widespread use of the advance text, reporters still will be required to cover speeches where no text is available, as well as press conferences where the speaker's comments are made in response to questions. To do this effectively, they must acquire some degree of skill in taking notes. Skillful note taking—at least from a journalistic point of view—goes well beyond stenography. Formal systems of shorthand may be helpful, and sooner or later every reporter develops his or her own method of abbreviated notation, but the key to taking good notes lies elsewhere. It has more to do with the ability to listen critically to what a speaker says.

The reporter who remains alert to the substance of the speaker's remarks and takes notes only on newsworthy remarks will find, in beginning to write the story, that already half the work has been done. The notes summarize the major points of the speech, and the only task remaining will be to construct a lead and develop an orderly story from those notes. If, on the other hand, the reporter functioned mainly as a stenographer, taking down comments without discretion, he or she will face the job of reviewing all of the notes and sorting out what is important before beginning to write.

Good writers do not waste time or energy. They listen for the significant comment or the telling phrase and then take notes. By eliminating trite or irrelevant material at this stage, they are ready to write when they return to their keyboards. Writers who train themselves to listen perceptively will discover how much more easily they remember the speaker's ideas without the aid of notes.

The kind of notes that writers find most useful are a skeletonized form of the ideas and comments they wish to record. They consist mainly of nouns and verbs, key words and phrases, with articles and prepositions omitted in the interest of speed. As long as there is no delay in getting to the writing stage, these fragments can be easily reconstituted into complete thoughts. When writers wish to quote a subject, they use quotation marks in their notes and take down the entire statement as accurately and completely as possible.

Many beginning reporters assume that note-taking skills no

longer matter in the electronic age. What they fail to realize is that while a tape recorder provides an accurate record of a speech, it does not eliminate note taking. A reporter who relies entirely on a tape recorder without taking notes must listen to the entire speech again—and take notes—after returning to the office. The tape recorder is most useful as a backup device to guarantee accuracy on important assignments. When used, it should be turned on, then ignored.

Taking notes and reporting speeches are skills that must be learned by practice. Certain aspects of the techniques were included here only because they are inseparably linked to the production of an accurate and coherent story.

SPEECH STORY STRUCTURE

In writing a story based on a speech, the journalist's objective is the same as in writing any other type of story: to focus on the news. Hence, the leads of most speech stories consist of a statement summarizing either the overall theme, if newsworthy, or a section of the speech that seems particularly significant.

In either case, the lead reflects what the writer sees as the most important aspect of the speech. One of the most common mistakes made by beginners in handling a speech story is to ignore the speaker's remarks altogether and build a lead on the circumstances of the speech, as in this example:

> Regina R. Busbee, a public opinion analyst, was the speaker last night at the annual membership meeting of the League of Women Voters of Rockville.

This lead is unacceptable simply because it contains no news; in fact, it could have been written the day before the event. In a speech story, the news is what the speaker said. If a speaker says nothing worth reporting, no story should be written.

Once a writer singles out the lead material, the next step is to cast it in a clear, emphatic form. With few exceptions, the most effective way to do this is by paraphrasing the speaker. The temptation always exists for journalists to let the speaker write the lead for them by using a direct quote. While this requires less effort, the result is often neither clear nor emphatic. Here is a typical example:

> "Fewer and fewer voters between the ages of 18 and 26 claim any allegiance to the two major political parties or to any party for that matter."
>
> This is the view of Regina R. Busbee, a public opinion analyst who last night addressed the annual membership meeting of the League of Women Voters of Rockville.

The above lead probably contains the angle that the writer wishes to emphasize. It was written to be part of a speech, however, and may not measure up to the more stringent requirements for a good news lead. If it does not, the fault lies not with the speaker but with the writer.

In any given address, the speaker's most interesting point may not be found in a single quotation. It might be implied by a series of remarks or by the speech as a whole. The specific task of the writer is to bring these ideas together for the reader. Thus, in the above example, a more enterprising writer might have written:

> A public opinion analyst has predicted that the growing sense of alienation among younger voters from established political parties will be a significant factor in electoral politics in the next decade.
>
> In a speech last night to the League of Women Voters of Rockville, Regina R. Busbee, a research analyst with Public Opinion Research Associates, said studies conducted by her firm during the past three years have shown a dramatic decline in party affiliation among voters in the 18 to 26 age group.
>
> "Prospective candidates who ignore these trends," she added, "will have little chance of success at the polls."
>
> Busbee also pointed out that . . .

Speech stories begin, therefore, with the most newsworthy aspect of the speech as summarized by the writer. If the speaker used unusually strong or colorful language to express these views, the writer may elect to quote certain words or phrases, as in this lead from *The Washington Post:*

> MANILA — A hardened Philippine bargaining position and caustic remarks about U.S. commitments in negotiating the future of U.S. military bases here risk offending Washington and causing "irreparable harm" to relations between the two countries, a U.S. special negotiator warned yesterday.

Once the main news angle has been expressed in the lead, the writer can begin an elaboration of this idea with paraphrase and direct quotes. If the speech contained other remarks approaching the lead in importance, the writer may wish to summarize these in the second paragraph before elaborating the lead. In overall development, the speech story follows the basic pattern of the inverted pyramid, with the more important remarks preceding those of lesser importance in a subtle interplay of paraphrase and direct quotation.

This *New York Times* report by Sam Howe Verhovek on an address given by Gov. Mario Cuomo of New York offers a good example of speech story structure:

> GETTYSBURG, Pa., Nov. 19 — On the 126th anniversary of the Gettysburg Address, Gov. Mario M. Cuomo said today that Lincoln never would have tolerated the "new slavery" of homelessness, drugs and despair or the "national tentativeness and political timidity" with which those problems are being met.
>
> Standing outdoors a few steps from where Lincoln delivered the 1863 speech that followed the bloodiest battle ever fought on American soil, the Governor repeatedly invoked the 16th President's words in a barely veiled attack on the Republicans who today claim Lincoln's mantle.
>
> While Mr. Cuomo avoided referring to political parties in his address at the ceremony sponsored by the Lincoln Fellowship of

Pennsylvania, he strongly implied that Lincoln might find his true home today in the Democratic Party. That effort seemed faintly reminiscent of Ronald Reagan's frequent embracing of the worlds of a President from outside his party, Franklin D. Roosevelt.

"I'd like to believe," Gov. Cuomo said of Lincoln, "that he'd take up the challenge of narrowing the gap between the haves and the have-nots in this society, of reuniting the two cities where Americans live today—one rich and glittering city on the hill, the other full of pain and despair and lost potential, the new slavery."

Of drug addiction and illiteracy, Mr. Cuomo said, "I'd like to believe Lincoln would chide a government whose response to this was tentative or timid or weak."

He denounced those who say society cannot afford that fight, "that 'we have the will but not the wallet.'" The reference was to President Bush's inaugural speech, in which he said the budget deficit meant the Government had "more will than wallet" for attacking the nation's social ills . . .

While the reporter's primary concern is the speech, at times circumstances surrounding the event may be more newsworthy than the speaker's remarks. The following lead from *The Washington Post* plays up that aspect of the story:

UNITED NATIONS, Oct. 19 — The United States, Britain and France today tried unsuccessfully to bar Jesse Jackson from giving a speech on Namibia to the General Assembly, claiming his remarks could jeopardize plans to hold elections in the South African-administered territory next month.

The journalist's job is to report the news, whether it comes from the speech itself, the audience's reaction to the speech or—as in the above example—an attempt to prevent the speaker from speaking.

The meeting story

One of the easiest ways for a prospective journalist to break into newspaper work is by covering suburban municipal meetings on a part-time basis. Major daily newspapers use full-time reporters to cover city hall, police and other regular beats, but the sheer number of municipalities surrounding the average American city makes coverage of local government in these areas an impossibility for the regular staff.

Consequently, most newspapers that attempt to provide suburban coverage—especially those with regional sections—use part-time reporters who are paid by the meeting. For the beginning journalist seeking an opportunity to develop reporting and writing skills, covering municipal and school board meetings is an ideal way to obtain it.

Meetings of government bodies, however, test a reporter's organizing skills because they consist of many unrelated actions that must be combined into one coherent story. While some metropolitan newspapers break their reports of city council sessions into separate stories by topic, the prevailing practice on most newspapers—daily and weekly—is to cover such meetings in one story.

This means that the reporter writing a meeting story faces two basic tasks: One is to decide which of all the different actions is important enough to be featured in the lead, and the other, to find a way to develop with some degree of order and continuity a story based on disparate information.

MEETING STORY LEADS

No simple formula exists for determining what aspect of a meeting should be spotlighted in the lead. Relevant criteria may be the number of people affected by a decision, the amount of money spent, or changes in existing policy. Generally speaking, actions that a public body takes assume more significance than actions proposed. But if a proposal is controversial, it could be lead material, as in this example from the Norristown (Pa.) *Times Herald:*

> In an effort to reduce district spending, the
> Norristown School District proposed to cut

> six sports programs at the middle and high
> school level last night.

Most meeting stories, however, focus on actions taken—as does this one, from the Doylestown (Pa.) *Intelligencer:*

> Warrington supervisors Tuesday night
> adopted updates to three residential zoning
> ordinances that, according to the board's
> chairman, will help people be better
> neighbors.

On occasion, after scanning notes from a meeting, reporters may find nothing that they think worth spotlighting in the lead. But a story must be written and a lead constructed. In such situations, the minimum requirement is that the material can be developed beyond the lead sentence. As they gain more experience in covering public affairs, reporters develop a feel for these kinds of judgments.

In writing leads and accounts of meetings, reporters should avoid unnecessary references to parliamentary procedure. They should write that city council "endorsed" a plan rather than "passed a resolution endorsing" it. Or say that the board "rejected" a proposal rather than "voted to reject" it. Unless essential to the issue at hand, the making and seconding of motions is generally ignored.

MEETING STORY STRUCTURE

If the structure of a typical meeting story were diagrammed, the resulting figure would be not one inverted pyramid but a stack of inverted pyramids, each one smaller than the one above. Unlike the normal inverted pyramid story, which concerns a single event, the meeting story covers a set of different stories connected only by the thread of the meeting.

This peculiar structure imposes two obligations on writers. First, as they move from topic to topic, they must write a new lead, or to put it another way, they must make sure that each part of the story is told in order of importance. Second, because there is so much unrelated information in reports of meetings, writers must use every available rhetorical device to give the story a semblance of continuity.

The first obligation seems simple enough. Still, beginning

reporters often forget, once they have left the lead material, that each succeeding topic should begin with the most significant aspect of that topic. When they do, they write story sections like this:

> Councilman Tom Edwards said he was concerned about the 30 m.p.h. speed limit in Elmwood Park.
>
> He said several area day-care centers were using the park for recess periods and that the number of children crossing park roads was creating a safety hazard. He recommended lowering the speed limit.
>
> Council voted to lower the speed limit to 20 m.p.h.

But since the rule about order of importance applies to each individual section, the above example should have taken this form:

> Council also lowered the speed limit in Elmwood Park from 30 to 20 m.p.h.
>
> The action was recommended by Councilman Tom Edwards, who noted that the increased use of the park by area day-care centers was creating a safety hazard.
>
> He said large numbers of children were crossing park roads at all times of the day.

Occasionally public meetings stick to just a single topic, which makes continuity easy for a writer, but most sessions of public bodies consist of widely divergent activity. This means that writers should try—as best they can—to glue the pieces together.

In switching topics, writers should look for connections that might be expressed in a transitional phrase, such as "In a related matter" or "In another attempt to deal with traffic problems." Obviously, if no connection exists, none can be created, so the writer might indicate the beginning of a new section by saying "In other business . . ." That phrase, however, should be used only once in a story, and at times the writer is forced to say simply "Council also . . ."

Rather than repeat this transition over and over at the end of a story, a reporter might write instead "Council also voted to," and then list each minor action in a phrase preceded by a dash or bullet. This device, called "shirttailing," is an effective way of handling miscellaneous information.

The following story taken from *The Post,* a community newspaper published in King of Prussia, Pa., provides readers with a well-organized, well-written report of a municipal meeting:

> A request to rezone an 8.9 acre Croton Woods tract to permit the construction of 52 townhouses was rejected this week by the Upper Merion Board of Supervisors.
>
> In a decision following a lengthy hearing on the request Monday night, the board heeded the wishes of area residents who said the development would both devalue their properties and burden area roads.
>
> Developer Robert G. Lee claimed there was "a local demand for this type of development," and that the townhouses would sell for more than $100,000 apiece.
>
> Board Chairman John W. O'Donnell had suggested that the supervisors take the request under advisement, but he was outvoted when Supervisor Abraham W. Martin called for an immediate vote on the issue.
>
> The property is currently zoned for residential development on at least one acre of property. The new zoning classification would have permitted six units an acre.
>
> In other business this week, the township announced that the police department will conduct a town watch meeting on Thursday night at 7:30 p.m. The presentation will include tips on preventing crime in the neighborhoods.
>
> Robert W. Geerdes, township manager, said that recently the township police department has apprehended several burglars and vandals because residents have notified the police of suspicious activities in their communities.
>
> In a related matter, the board voted to increase the fee it charges to businesses and residents for police responses to private burglar alarms. The fee was increased from $10 a call to $35.

Geerdes said about 125 alarms are connected to the township dispatcher facility.

The board also voted to amend its application to the U.S. Department of Housing and Urban Development so that it can use a partial grant to straighten out a dogleg on Summit Street in Swedeland. There was no cost estimate for the work.

The board also accepted bids for exterior repairs to be made to the township community center on Moore Road. The work will involve installation of a metal roof, exterior wall painting and masonry repairs and will be funded by a 90 percent federal grant.

The township administration will make recommendations on the acceptance of the bids next month.

In this story the writer fulfilled both obligations to the reader. The story follows order of importance and each section is itself a miniature inverted pyramid. In addition, the writer clearly marked each shift of topic and made connections between topics wherever possible.

The obituary

Many newspaper readers do not know the difference between an obituary and a death notice. They are unaware that an obituary is a news story and that a death notice is a form of classified advertising paid for by the funeral director and billed to the survivors. Beginning journalists—especially on smaller newspapers—learn the difference quickly since they may write several obituaries a day.

Who rates an obituary? The answer is relative to each individual newspaper. Small community newspapers usually try to publish obituaries of all deceased residents in their circulation area. Metropolitan newspapers, for reasons of space, must be more selective; a minimum level of prominence is required for the deceased to get an obituary.

In any event, an obituary is a news story and it should be treated like one. This means that it should have an emphatic lead and be developed in a way that makes it interesting to read. Unfortunately, too many newspapers treat obituaries as little more than death notices and apply a standard writing formula that makes no distinctions among the deceased.

While most often applied to news of death, the obituary structure can also be used for news of awards, honors and appointments. Both kinds of stories begin with the news, then reconstruct the subject's life up to that point. One obvious difference is that in an obituary the writer can speak with the ultimate degree of finality about the subject.

OBITUARY LEADS

It might seem odd to say that obituaries should have emphatic leads. But obituaries are news stories, and the news is that a particular person has died. To be emphatic, the lead must clearly identify the deceased in a way that would be recognizable to friends and associates. Beginning an obituary in the following manner is really an insult to the deceased:

> Frank Garcia, a former resident of Greensburg, died yesterday at the Fairview Nursing Home in Caldwell after a long illness. He was 77.

This lead indicates that the writer did not bother to find out anything that would have given the deceased a specific identity in the last story that would ever be written about him. It would not have taken much effort to write a lead like this:

> Frank Garcia, a former Greensburg resident who operated a bicycle repair shop on Main Street for 35 years, died yesterday at the Fairview Nursing Home in Caldwell. He was 77.

Thus, the key to effective obituary leads is accurate identification of the deceased. In most cases, the writer can compose an identifying phrase after a careful reading of the information supplied by the funeral director. With a prominent subject, further investigation may be necessary, and the resulting lead identity may be a composite of both professional and civic roles, as in this example from *The New York Times:*

> Joseph G. Blum, a New York lawyer for more than six decades and long-time benefactor of people with disabilities, died on Sunday at his home in Larchmont, N.Y. He was 86 years old.

Here a dual identity was necessary to adequately identify the deceased to those who knew him. When a writer is dealing with a subject of extreme prominence, with accomplishments in several fields, choosing an accurate and effective identification may be the most difficult part of the obituary process. An Associated Press writer faced just such a task in writing the lead for an obituary of the Australian musician Peter Allen:

> NEW YORK — Peter Allen, the Australian singer, dancer, songwriter and pianist, who was discovered by Judy Garland and once married to her daughter Liza Minelli, died yesterday in San Diego. He was 48.

In preparing obituaries of women who did not have professional careers, writers should avoid the once-common practice of identifying the deceased only with reference to her husband—or even dead husband—as in this lead:

> Ernestine Miller, widow of the Rev. Paul M. Miller, died yesterday at her home in Maple Glen. She was 87.

An alert writer who took the time to examine Mrs. Miller's background information would have written a lead like this one:

> Ernestine Miller, a former president of the Montgomery County Branch of the American Red Cross who was long active in charitable activities, died yesterday at her home in Maple Glen. She was 87.

In addition to the name and identity, obituary leads should include the time and place of death. The cause of death, if it can be determined, and the age of the deceased may also be mentioned.

OBITUARY DEVELOPMENT

"Formula" obituaries that fail to adequately identify the deceased in the lead usually fall down in development as well. Their second paragraph almost always begins this way: "Born in 1920 . . ." The rest of the material consists of a chronological listing of information.

As news stories, obituaries must be ordered by importance. The best place to start is with the identity that has been highlighted in the lead. If the deceased has been described in the lead as "a widely known trial lawyer," then the writer should begin development with material to support that description. If the deceased was "an advocate for fair housing practices," development should lead off with the ways this advocacy was expressed.

Once that aspect of the subject's life has been fully covered, then the writer can continue to the next—always following order of importance. While graduation from college is important in most people's lives, rarely does it rank as their most important accomplishment in retrospect. Memberships in clubs and organizations are important in a formal way but not nearly as significant as the things the deceased has *done.*

Consequently, this material is held for later paragraphs in the story and grouped according to kind, with professional memberships separated from memberships in social or fraternal organizations. The last two paragraphs of the obituary usually are reserved for survivors and funeral arrangements, and here the writer simply follows the newspaper's own style for handling this information.

The best obituaries offer readers not only an accurate summary of the subject's life, but also a feeling for the subject as a person. They do this by including—whenever possible—anecdotal material, quotes from the subject, comments from friends and colleagues, and descriptive writing along with factual information.

In an obituary of Harry Reasoner, the renowned television journalist, the *Philadelphia Inquirer* noted that it was Reasoner's broadcast writing that first attracted attention, then included a particularly effective example:

> When comedian Ernie Kovacs was killed in an automobile accident in 1962, Mr. Reasoner closed a newscast with the observation:
>
> "Somebody dies in an unprepared hurry, and you are touched with a dozen quick and recent memories: the sweetness of last evening, the uselessness of a mean word or an undone promise. It could be you, with all those untidy memories of recent days never to be straightened out. There's a shiver in the sunlight, touching the warmth of life that you've been reminded you hold only for a moment."

The quote is effective because it reveals the man as well as the writer. Reasoner, of course, was a national figure, but even obituaries of less prominent persons deserve careful writing. In another *Inquirer* obituary for one of its own staff members, sports editor Frank Dolson used the second paragraph to characterize a colleague:

> Alex Rosen, 88, whose career as a sportswriter in this city spanned seven decades, died Friday in Fairfield, Conn.
>
> Mr. Rosen, who wrote a bowling column in The Inquirer for the last 30 years, was the antithesis of what has come to be known as the typical Philadelphia sportswriter. Through all of his working years and the thousands of stories he wrote, it's doubtful he ever said or wrote an unkind word about anyone.

Obituary structure can also be used in stories that report on significant achievements in a subject's life. In this example from the *Los Angeles Times,* the news is retirement:

> The dean of America's police reporters ended his career Friday the way he started it 56 years ago—in a chaotic police pressroom chasing a story that sent shock waves across Los Angeles.

> Norman "Jake" Jacoby left his City News
> Service desk at the Los Angeles Police
> Department headquarters for the last time
> after filing dozens of bulletins, stories and
> updates on Friday's earthquake for area radio
> and TV stations and newspapers.
>
> It was just another day at the office for
> Jacoby, 75. Since 1935, he has pounded out
> stories of mayhem, murders and madmen
> stalking the streets of Los Angeles that not
> even Raymond Chandler could have thought
> up . . .

The story, by Bob Pool, goes on to recapitulate Jacoby's
experiences as a police reporter and includes—as good obituaries
do—quotes from those who knew the subject well:

> Despite his rapport with police, Jacoby
> broke dozens of stories about scandal in the
> Police Department.
>
> "There were times I would have liked to
> put a gag on him that would have taken an
> army to take off," said Deputy Chief William
> Booth, a former press relations officer who
> worked for 14 years with Jacoby. "He's a
> legend in journalism, and to the LAPD also.
> We named the pressroom after him about
> seven years ago."

Pool ends the story strongly with a direct quote from Jacoby:

> A steady stream of police and Parker
> Center workers said goodby. Computer
> operator Anita Rouse gave the reporter a hug
> and was posing arm in arm with him for a
> snapshot when the temblor struck.
>
> "I went out with a pretty girl shaking in my
> arms," the great-grandfather quipped. "You
> can't do better than that."

In the hands of a skillful writer, the obituary form can be used
to generate reader interest whether the subject is dead or alive.

7 News in Context

THE 20TH CENTURY has been the setting for the greatest expansion of communications technology in human history. It began modestly enough with a wireless version of the telegraph that linked ships to the mainland and enhanced newspaper coverage of sporting events. In less than two decades, however, this innocuous device—reincarnated as radio—would shatter the news monopoly of the printing press and set off a chain reaction of invention culminating in what is commonly referred to as the "electronic revolution."

Evidence of this revolution surrounds us in the form of broadcast and cable television, video cameras, magnetic and digital recorders, computer networks and satellite transmitters. The net effect is that never before has so much news and information been available to so many people. While we tend to believe that with communications, "more is better," some observers question the long-term political and social effects of this phenomenon.

One of the first critics to challenge the conventional wisdom was Jacques Ellul, the French social historian, who has expressed concern about the proliferation of news by mass media and its effect on the ability of citizens and their leaders to make sound political decisions.

In his book *The Political Illusion,* a provocative study of contemporary political institutions, Ellul argues that "the predominance of news produces a fundamental political incapacity in the individual." This condition, he says, is brought on by an overdose of diverse and discontinuous information: "In order not to drown in this incessant flow, man is forced to forget."

This forgetting, Ellul points out, has profound significance in political life:

> There is no politics where there is no grasp of the past, where there is no continuity, where there is no analysis of errors or capacity to understand the present through that analysis and in that continuity. But current events obscure everything, even for the specialists. Current news pre-empts the sense of continuity, prevents the use of memory, and leads to a constant falsification of past events when they are evoked again in the stream of news.

Closer to home, W. Lance Bennett, a professor of political science at the University of Washington and a noted media analyst, raises similar questions about the flood of discontinuous information produced by contemporary mass media. In his similarly titled book *News: The Politics of Illusion,* Bennett declares:

> Most news stories, as currently conceived, refract the everyday real world into free-floating particles of dubious meaning. In this refraction process, events resulting from the same political or economic forces are often treated as though they were independent. Long-term trends and historical patterns are seldom made part of the news because they are hard to tell as simple stories. Events spring full-blown, from out of nowhere, into the headlines. In place of seeing a coherent world anchored in clear historical, economic, and political tendencies, the public is exposed to a world driven into chaos by seemingly arbitrary and mysterious forces.

These comments may be unsettling to journalists who, like many of their readers, believe that being well informed is a state similar to being well educated. But overemphasis on the value of information, while it helps to increase the audience for news media, blurs the critical distinction between the simple amassing of factual data and *understanding,* which is the ability to relate facts to each other in some meaningful way.

Both commentators point out that electronic media have heightened the emphasis on immediacy in contemporary political affairs. Ellul agrees that it is exciting to watch political leaders and their activities via television, but he warns viewers:

> These are false political problems because they are always appearances only, visible consequences, manifestations of deeper and more decisive problems from which the citizen living in the news turns away because they are not as exciting as the latest speech.

Bennett adds that the "action news" of electronic media "often tries to imitate 'analysis' by trading in the story format for news collages, called 'clusters' in radio and television, which contain many images with few coherent connections."

By their very nature, electronic media are captives of immediacy, for until a problem has taken tangible form, as an event or spectacle, it cannot be recorded or videotaped. Consequently, in the electronic age, the primary responsibility for putting news into a meaningful framework falls upon the print journalist. Of all media, it is the printed word that is best suited to making the public aware of the significant currents that run well below the agitated surface of events. In print, the relevant past can more easily be combined with present data to suggest a feasible future.

To keep Ellul's "citizen living in the news" from turning away from the important but nonspectacular message, print journalists today will need to master a galaxy of skills in addition to writing and reporting. How effectively they meet this challenge may well determine the future of democratic political life in America, for as novelist Mary McCarthy noted in her book *The Mask of State: Watergate Portraits:*

> Printer's ink and domestic liberty have an old association. Whereas television, being a mass medium, can be controlled and manipulated, total control of the printed word, as has been demonstrated in the Soviet Union, seems to be all but impossible. If newspapers are censored or suppressed, broadsides and leaflets can still circulate, passing from hand to hand.

It might appear from all of the above that the job of putting news in a wider context is reserved for a select group of writers charged with analyzing national or foreign affairs. Nothing could be further from the truth. The task of piecing together those fragments that are the raw material of meaningful news falls on every journalist in every area of reporting.

Making connections

The simplest and most fundamental relationship that can exist between two news items is that both are parts of a larger story. This relationship can be readily observed in sequential stories about a continuing event, such as a major criminal trial, but it is present whenever a story relates to some prior news event, regardless of the time span intervening. It is the journalist's duty to discover such relationships and make them clear to the reader.

Problems of identification were illustrated in Chapter 2 by using the example of a boy who died from injuries received two weeks earlier in a playground accident. The accident itself, in which a boy was critically injured, was a news story, and the death of an 8-year-old boy also is news, if only an obituary. Yet the second story offers no real meaning to the reader unless it is related to the first. Here, the connection between the stories is hard to miss. The real challenge to journalists is to find relationships that are not as obvious and that require some effort to uncover.

There are no hard and fast rules for finding hidden relationships between stories, but success comes most often to reporters who invest time and energy in the process. Undoubtedly the major success story of our time is that of Carl Bernstein and Bob Woodward, the former *Washington Post* reporters whose dogged persistence in running down leads ultimately produced the Watergate revelations.

Few journalists, of course, will have an opportunity to unearth a story of this magnitude. Still, every story that suggests a relationship to other events should be checked out with the basic research tools of the reporter: clipping files, public records and interviews. Not to follow through when a relationship is suggested makes the writer a perpetrator of the kind of discontinuity that the authors cited earlier in this chapter find so debilitating to political life.

Having established a connection between events, the writer must express it clearly for the reader. Where a simple relationship to an earlier story exists, the linkage—or "tie-back," as it is called in the newsroom—should be spelled out in the lead, as in this example from *The Boston Globe:*

> DEDHAM — Kenneth G. Seguin, the software executive charged with the April bludgeoning death of his wife, was indicted yesterday in the murders of his two children, whose bodies were found in a Franklin pond three days after their mother's body was discovered floating in the Sudbury River.

In the case of a "running story"—a story that appears daily about a continuing news event—the tie-back becomes a standardized paragraph inserted after the day's news has been elaborated. The writer assumes that the reader has seen some of the preceding accounts.

An example of such a story was the 1992 perjury trial of a former deputy director of the Central Intelligence Agency. The trial received nationwide media attention, yet even after three weeks of daily reports focusing on the testimony of witnesses, the Associated Press made sure that recapitulation appeared high in its stories. One story began this way:

> WASHINGTON — A federal judge threatened to hold Clair E. George in contempt yesterday after the former CIA spy chief repeatedly interrupted the prosecutor while testifying in his Iran-contra trial.

The next five paragraphs describe the events leading up to the judge's threat, then the necessary information is provided:

> The judicial threat came as George closed 2½ days of testimony in his own defense. The former chief of CIA overseas spy operations has pleaded not guilty to three counts of obstructing Congress and a federal grand jury, and six counts of perjury and making false statements.

Newswriters cannot assume too much about the reader's prior knowledge. Except for continuing stories of major significance, enough material must be included from earlier accounts to make the story completely understandable to first-time readers. Recapitulation may require more than one paragraph, but as the event progresses, earlier material is condensed sharply to make room for more recent background information.

A *New York Times* story about the latest development arising from the midair explosion of a Pan American World Airways jetliner over Lockerbie, Scotland, nearly four years earlier, began this way:

> A jury decided yesterday that Pan American World Airways was liable for damages because its security procedures failed to protect passengers in the 1988 explosion of Flight 103 over Lockerbie, Scotland, a bombing that took 270 lives.

The next five paragraphs explain the implications of the verdict and the plaintiffs' reactions. Paragraph six provides the recapitulation:

> The Lockerbie explosion, attributed to a terrorist bomb planted in a suitcase, blew up a Boeing 747 jetliner heading from London to New York on Dec. 21, 1988. All 259 people on the plane were killed, along with 11 more on the ground. The issue in dispute at the trial was whether Pan Am could be held liable in the lawsuits filed by the families of more than 200 of the passengers.

Even though this disaster was heavily publicized when it occurred and was in and out of the news since that time, the writer included enough information to refresh the memories of readers who probably had some knowledge of the original event. In follow-up stories where background information is not extensive, the writer may choose to weave it into the new material and avoid breaking the flow of the news.

Providing context

In the previous section, a news story was shown to be meaningless when not clearly linked to prior related events. There are other ways, however, in which news can be rendered meaningless. Even stories with no relation to previous news events can be without meaning for readers if the writer fails to provide information that—while not a part of the immediate story—is necessary for its understanding.

Such information is essential for reporting the activities of public bodies like city councils or school boards. For a reporter to write that a proposed ordinance has been referred to a particular committee is meaningless. Every city hall reporter soon learns that one committee may mean sudden death for a bill while another may speed its passage. Unless the reporter shares this information with the reader, the story is incomplete.

All complicated documents, such as proposed ordinances or statutes, budget messages and reports of investigatory committees become meaningful when placed within a broader context. Reporters who simply pass on summaries of these documents, without analyzing their significance or suggesting possible implications, serve no real purpose and become, in the words of columnist Pete Hamill, "clerks of fact."

Even something as simple as a proposed ordinance ought to generate a series of questions in the reporter's mind: Why is it being proposed? Was it ever proposed before? If it was, why was it rejected? Do other municipalities have similar ordinances? What effect will it have on the community? In trying to find the answers, the writer adds context to the news.

But putting news in context is not solely the responsibility of the public affairs reporter. Every newswriter comes across stories whose meaning would be enhanced by five minutes of research in an encyclopedia or almanac or by a telephone call to a local authority on the subject. This practice is not a writing skill but a habit of mind, a critical stance that enables the writer to get on top of the material and ask the kinds of questions that will produce a meaningful story.

The ability to take an isolated news item or press release and fill in the missing information from personal research or telephone interviews is as much of an asset to contemporary journalists as the ability to write clear and forceful prose. It is a particularly useful skill for writers on weekly newspapers, where stories that received superficial coverage by the dailies can be adequately researched and given a fresh and more comprehensive presentation.

Localizing news

One of the most frequent criticisms made of newspapers is that most of their stories hold little or no meaning for the average reader. This charge is not wholly without foundation, as even a brief examination of many dailies will demonstrate. Judging by the kind of stories that make up the front page or that command the boldest headlines and the greatest amount of space, it seems that the potential to shock, titillate or entertain the reader figures heavily in determining news values.

The problem with this kind of news—even though it helps to sell newspapers—is that it does not provide readers with the kind of information they need to participate in a democratic society. When sensational or entertaining news predominates in newspapers, it trivializes the role of the press and turns readers into spectators— which is not what the Founding Fathers had in mind when they drafted the First Amendment. Press freedom was built into the Constitution because it was understood to be a necessary adjunct to a democratic government.

It makes no sense to say that a system of government puts power in the hands of the people if the people have no way of finding out what goes on. In the early history of the press, newspapers were censored by monarchs who believed—and rightly so—that an informed populace threatened their power. Even today, public officials disturbed by news media that carry out their First Amendment role aggressively often try to curb the press. But the greatest threat to press freedom may come from newspapers that fail to provide readers with the kind of useful information they need to obtain a greater degree of control over their lives, their environment and the institutions that claim to serve them.

Sensationalism is not the only problem. Newspapers that allot a disproportionate amount of space to stories about international affairs and provide repetitious coverage of national politics also cast readers in the role of spectators and confirm their growing sense of powerlessness. Rather than overwhelm readers with news of events over which they have little or no control, newspapers should give high priority to stories that enable readers to participate in areas where their involvement can make a difference.

Obtaining such stories, however, requires intelligent and energetic local reporting. It is easier—and cheaper—to download wire service stories from the computer than to provide competent local coverage. But if serving readers is a priority, there is no choice.

These, of course, are editorial decisions, but writers also play a role. In handling wire service copy, they should try to make the news more meaningful for readers by pointing out any regional implications. Such implications are not always apparent and may require the writer to check with local authorities or regional representatives of federal and state agencies, but the resulting story usually brings the news into sharper focus. Even when national news clearly relates to the area, the connections must be spelled out in detail by local reporters.

In the following story the Washington Bureau of the *Des Moines Register* analyzed Census Bureau data from Iowa to provide readers with a meaningful contrast to national figures:

> Remember the stories about elderly couples eating dog food? The heart-breaking tales of a grandmother packed off to the county home?
>
> One of the quiet successes of the war on poverty is that these stories are becoming increasingly rare. Among older Iowans, the poverty rate went from 28.3 percent in 1969 to 11.2 percent in 1989, according to the census.
>
> The young were not so fortunate. Overall, 17.5 percent of all preschool children in Iowa were living in poverty in 1989, up from 11 percent two decades earlier. In Waterloo, nearly one-third of all preschoolers were in poverty. In Davenport it's 29 percent.
>
> Both developments mirror national statistics, which show the elderly poverty rate has declined to 12.8 percent while the preschool rate has risen to 20.1 percent . . .

The difference between this story and a wire service account that could appear in any newspaper is obvious. Newspapers without Washington bureaus can add relevant material to the wire story or prepare an accompanying "sidebar" story on local aspects. Weekly newspapers can use all of this material as the basis for a comprehensive feature on the subject.

To stress localization of news is not to champion journalistic provincialism. It is simply a way of making news more meaningful by emphasizing its connection to the reader. A strong editorial bias in favor of locally relevant news also acts as a deterrent to the indiscriminate use of wire copy as filler.

Using background

Up to this point the term "background" has been used to mean the kind of factual information that a reader needs to fully understand a story. It can range from basic information, such as the proper names, ages, occupations and addresses of persons involved in news events, to the kinds of information referred to in the preceding sections—information which almost always must be obtained by reporters who ask the right questions.

Another kind of background information goes well beyond filling gaps in the story; it changes the ultimate character of the story itself. Many of the stories that appear in newspapers are ephemeral, with little or no significance other than what information they contain. Other stories have broader implications because of a possible history or connection to other events. The latter type offers alert reporters an opportunity to explore these connections and, in many cases, produce another story that is different and far more meaningful to the reader than the original story.

Take, for example, a story about a fatal traffic accident. The reporter, in checking her information, recalls writing a story about another fatal accident at the same intersection less than six months ago. She writes the story for today's newspaper, then goes to the newspaper's library and checks the bound volumes of the paper. Sure enough, a fatality did occur at that spot and the circumstances are amazingly similar. The reporter goes back to her desk and calls the police chief, asking him about that intersection. He says that there have been four or five fatalities there since he joined the force.

The reporter is curious. She gets in her car and drives to the intersection. As she approaches the intersection from the same street as the accident victims, she notices that because of a steep incline in the road approaching from her left, visibility is less than 35 yards. Now the reporter has information for a new story that might help to explain why the previous accidents occurred.

This somewhat elementary example helps to explain what is meant by the use of background information to create stories. While the background here is not necessary for writing the original story, it enables the writer to produce another and far more significant account. Using background in this way is an essential requirement for producing "developed" stories—the next topic.

Developing news

Up to this point in the chapter, discussion has centered on stories based on newsworthy events, acts of public bodies, documents or previous news stories. Yet some of the most important articles that a journalist can write arise from material that originates outside the news stream.

Reporters who wait for stories to "break," that is, force their way into the news through violent acts, public demonstrations, litigation and the like, always remain at the mercy of events. The real story, as already noted, often lies well below the visible event. But many important stories never become visible at all until brought into public view by an enterprising and imaginative journalist.

This kind of story evolves not from events or from other news but from the effort and ingenuity of the writer. The best of these stories often receive Pulitzer Prizes for investigative reporting; all of them offer writers the unique satisfaction that comes from having "made news."

To readers, "developed" stories appear to have come from nowhere, but the experienced journalist knows that they can spring from a variety of sources. Many begin with rumors or tips from sources outside the newspaper. Others may turn up while the writer is researching one story and comes across material that somehow "doesn't add up"; in the attempt to check out the discrepancy, he or she may find another story. Some of the best developed stories arise simply from the feeling of an alert reporter that something is wrong or that there must be some explanation for a peculiar set of circumstances.

Regardless of the original source, the developed story takes its final shape from the painstaking research of the reporter who lets no rumor pass unchecked nor accepts as fact any information that he or she has not personally verified. Preparing such a story can be a time-consuming and laborious process, and it may take weeks or even months before the final pieces fall into place. Nonetheless, a well-written and carefully researched developed story is news in the most meaningful sense of the word.

While daily newspapers are usually better equipped—in terms of staff and resources—for investigatory journalism, weeklies willing to invest the time and effort required will find that these stories offer them an opportunity to hold their own against the more routine coverage of local affairs that is often required of the daily press.

After a five-month investigation of the testing and promotion of chlorofluorocarbons by the Du Pont Co., Merritt Wallick, a reporter for the Wilmington (Del.) *News Journal,* produced a series of articles that raised significant questions about the safety of these chemicals and corporate responsibility. Wallick examined internal Du Pont memos and thousands of pages of records, questioned Du Pont officials for more than 20 hours and conducted more than 100 other interviews.

His first article began as follows:

> When Standard Manufacturing Co. contacted the Du Pont Co. in 1986 on behalf of a pregnant employee who routinely breathed solvent Freon 113 on the job, it was assured by Du Pont officials the woman had nothing to fear.
>
> Du Pont never told anyone at the Dallas plant that its own expert believed Du Pont's study on Freon 113 and birth defects was flawed.
>
> Fielding a 1979 inquiry from the automobile industry, Du Pont kept silent on test results linking Freon 113 to cancer. For decades, Du Pont made a habit of saying as

little as possible on the dangers of Freon 113.

Indeed, for 50 years Du Pont has assured a world hungry for Freon 113 that the prized chemical was safe—nearly as harmless as water. Those assurances, however, often skirted the truth and may have contributed to the deaths of scores of workers who used Freon 113.

A five-month investigation by The News Journal has revealed that Du Pont never has had sufficient evidence to justify the safety claims it widely made about the popular solvent, today used primarily in the electronics industry. But it had ample evidence of the chemical's dangers . . .

Not all developed stories are aimed at exposing questionable activities, as this *Denver Post* feature by Janet Bingham illustrates:

When she graduated as 1989 valedictorian from Aguilar High School in Southern Colorado, Lisa Coca had nearly an A average.

But when she arrived at Trinidad State Junior College, she was placed in remedial math.

Classmate Patricia Gonzalez, who had earned A's and B's and ranked third in the same class of 21, thought she was good at English and history—until she got to Trinidad State.

"My written papers came back all marked up, telling me my sentence structure was awkward and paragraphing bad," she said. "In history, I didn't even know what the Renaissance was. I thought it was a festival in Colorado Springs."

Both say they were cheated out of a good high school education. "I want to go back and tell the students there now, 'You have to do more than what's expected of you here, a lot more,'" said Gonzalez. "I'm still trying to play catch-up."

More than 30,000 Colorado high school students will receive high school diplomas this spring. But while graduation is still a day of

> pride, many are questioning what the diploma
> really means . . .

Of all forms of journalism, the developed story offers reporters maximum control over their own material. As writers, they can function not merely as transmitters of information whose value has been established elsewhere but as originators and judges of meaningful news.

8 "Featurizing" the News

WHENEVER REPORTERS write stories under deadline conditions—which is most of the time—they use the inverted pyramid or one of its variations. They use this structure because it is a prefabricated news container that can be expanded or contracted like an accordion to fit the time and space available to the story.

Yet the very qualities that make the inverted pyramid so useful for spot news reporting against deadlines limit its effectiveness for other types of stories. In addition to hard news, which is event-centered and serious, newspapers also publish lighter stories that make up for their lack of importance with humor, irony or human interest. Still other stories may address serious topics, but they do so from a wider perspective than yesterday's events. Applying the inverted pyramid form to stories like these simply does not work.

Newspapers publish humorous stories to entertain readers and offset serious news. But in constructing such stories, writers find themselves in the same position as a stand-up comedian telling a joke. If they want to maximize the humor, they must generate suspense and save something for the end. The inverted pyramid form puts the punch line at the beginning.

As news stories move away from single events and attempt to focus on the significance of an issue, the kind of material that generates interest in inverted pyramid leads—such as conflict, violence or death—may not be available to the writer. To catch the reader's attention in these kinds of stories, the journalist dips into the fiction writer's bag of tricks and uses contrast, paradox, anecdotes, description and dialogue.

Thus, in journalism as in architecture, form follows function. For handling hard news in a narrow time frame under deadline pressure, the inverted pyramid is a useful and effective structure. When the purpose of the story is to analyze a situation, provide historical perspective or entertain the reader, then the structure must be modified to fit the purpose.

Traditional alternatives

Prior to the 1960s, the distinction between news and features was much sharper than it is today. "News" referred to serious stories about crime, politics or disaster; "features" were anything else, but mainly human interest stories designed to entertain or amuse the reader. Pressure from electronic media—especially television—helped to blur that distinction, as newspaper editors slowly realized that the feature form applied to hard news topics provided information that TV news usually did not offer.

But in the pretelevision newsroom the choice was clear—and limited! Except for the fully developed feature, which as soft news was relegated to the back sections of the paper, the only alternatives available to writers were short feature items, called "page brighteners" or "brights," and the longer "sidebars," which accompanied serious news to add a human interest dimension.

PAGE BRIGHTENERS

When radio appeared as a dynamic news medium during the 1920s, it created a demand in the daily press for short, human interest items to brighten columns of type that by contrast seemed sober and monotonous. Aware that such material was rarely obtainable in sufficient quantity at the local level and sensing a potential market, both the Associated Press and the United Press (as it was then called) urged their bureaus to keep watch for unusual stories. Short features in rough form would be sent to New York headquarters where staff members with a flair for this kind of copy rewrote them for the national wires.

From the 1930s on—except for those periods when war news and casualty lists filled all available news space—human interest items from the wires could be found scattered throughout American daily newspapers. In these stories writers cast aside the inverted pyramid and structured information to fit the story.

Here is an early example from the Associated Press in 1930:

> YONKERS, N.Y., Nov. 23 (A.P.) — The executive type stick-up man went to work (with a gun) in a restaurant early today. He issued orders to the manager, George Van Sork.
>
> "Put down that milk," he commanded. Van Sork did, without a word.
>
> "Get over that counter." Van Sork did, saying nothing.
>
> "Shove those dishes back." It was done without comment.
>
> "Give me your money." It was $22.40, and Van Sork handed it over, still without a word.
>
> The stick-up man backed toward the door.
>
> "Don't move," he ordered, "until you hear my motor start.
>
> "And," he added, "the next time you're held up don't talk so much."

If the writing style of these early stories seems awkward by comparison to contemporary examples, the writers nevertheless were establishing structural patterns that would be used for the rest of the century. They leaned heavily on the narrative, suspended interest, and dialogue, and strove for clever, unconventional leads that would excite the reader's curiosity, as does this example from the United Press in 1953:

> TOKYO, Nov. 21 (UP) — Japanese railroad engineers want a raise in pay so badly that they just have to let off a little steam.
>
> They decided to do it all together at noon next Wednesday. They will blow the whistles of 5,000 locomotives for one full minute.
>
> The engineers chapter of the National

Railway Workers Union said this will cost the government, which operates the railroads, 130 yen (about 30 cents) per engine, or the equivalent of $1,500.

An Associated Press story from the same year is a classic example of the suspended interest technique:

> SOUTH BEND, Ind., Nov. 25 (AP) — When Paul Hayn left home this morning to take his wife to the maternity ward in Osteopathic Hospital he thought he knew where the hospital was.
>
> He drove the 25 miles from Walkerton, southwest of South Bend, through the south side section where the hospital is and pulled up in front of the MarMain Arms apartment on the far north side. He escorted his wife into the ornate lobby before he discovered his error. Then it was too late to get back to the hospital.
>
> His wife, Dorothy, 25, gave birth to a daughter in the apartment house lobby. The mother and baby were taken in a police car to near-by Memorial Hospital where both were reported in good condition.

At first glance, the above story appears to be a simple chronology, but the writer has created suspense in the lead by using the phrase "he thought he knew where the hospital was." This signals the reader that something unusual happened.

Short human interest features from the wire services became models for alternative structure, and newswriters across the country copied the styles whenever an opportunity presented itself. Those opportunities were rare; except for stylistic experiments in a handful of tabloids, few daily newspapers prior to the 1960s applied imaginative writing techniques to the news. One notable—and surprising—exception was *The New York Times,* which frequently featurized local news stories with humorous possibilities. This one, from the *Times* in 1946, was a natural:

> This is a story with several morals, the first of which is: Don't call the police for your

neighbors's piano-playing guest when the pianist is the police captain's wife. Also, if you think music is noise, don't seek sympathy from Magistrate J. Roland Sala.

The tale, which ran its course in Flatbush Court yesterday, began in Brooklyn on Feb. 9. That night Timothy Collins got worked up in his small stucco-frame house at 1365 Brooklyn Avenue, Brooklyn. He did not like the piano music coming from the adjoining house of William L. McMahon. Besides it was keeping his children awake.

First he called his neighbor, then the police. The police quickly learned that the pianist was Mrs. Vera Harkins, wife of Walter Harkins, police captain at the Borough Park police station, Brooklyn. They did nothing. But Mr. McMahon, now an irate host, obtained a summons charging Mr. Collins with disorderly conduct . . .

Wire services still supply these stories, but they now appear more frequently in specialty columns rather than by themselves because of the current emphasis on a unified layout with fewer page elements. This one, from "The Scene" column of the *Philadelphia Inquirer,* indicates how little the form has changed in five decades:

John Lester awoke to some real bad news the other day.

Police and paramedics in Beacon, N.Y., jostled him and told him he'd just been run over by a train. Lester, 31, yawned.

His would-be rescuers responded to a report of a man hit by a train and found Lester unhurt and unconscious on the Metro-North Commuter Rail line.

The train rumbled over him while he slept soundly—and safely.

"Talk about a sound sleeper!" said police Lt. William Cornett. "I mean, these aren't like the old trains, but they do make a considerable amount of noise."

Police took Lester to a hospital for evaluation.

In case you're wondering: Yes, he was drunk, according to police.

Newspapers will continue to use such stories as long as editors believe that readers need an occasional break from the heavy dose of suffering, death and disaster that accompanies most serious news.

SIDEBARS

The traditional feature form that came closest to the contemporary news feature was the sidebar, the human interest adjunct of the major news story. While shorter than full-length features and focused on human interest aspects of newsworthy events, sidebars nevertheless followed normal feature style, with anecdotal leads, narrative structure, vivid writing and numerous direct quotes. In disaster situations, such as in the following *Houston Post* story by Tom Olmstead that accompanied a news account of the 1959 fire and explosions aboard an oil tanker docked at Houston, Texas, even first-person reports are acceptable:

> HOUSTON, Tex., Nov. 8 (AP) — From 100 yards away the scene at the dockside where the Amoco Virginia was burning looked something like a movie I once saw, "Dante's Inferno."
>
> Small figures milled back and forth in the flickering orange light from billowing flames amidships.
>
> Firemen, bent low as they tugged writhing lengths of hose, looked like gnomes in the heart of Hell.
>
> Moving closer I could feel the fierce heat and smell the oily smoke. I could also hear firemen with smudged faces grumbling about low water pressure.
>
> Someone explained that a water pump had broken down earlier in the day and had not been repaired at the time the explosion rocked the tanker.
>
> Back a few yards, ambulance men were transferring an injured man from one stretcher to another.
>
> His eyes were glazed with shock but the man did manage to mumble his name, Leonard C. Crisp, before pain closed his mouth . . .

Such stories provide a vivid alternative to the main account and take readers behind the statistics to see events in concrete, human terms. Even in the age of electronic journalism, the sidebar remains a useful news form because a reporter can often go where camera crews cannot. This *Philadelphia Inquirer* sidebar, written by Andrew Maykuth and Jeffrey Fleishman to accompany the paper's main story on the fiery destruction in 1993 of the Branch Davidian compound near Waco, Texas, follows the traditional sidebar pattern:

> WACO, Texas — The end began with a phone call.
>
> A few minutes before dawn, the phone that had been the vehicle for thousands of hours of fruitless negotiation rang one final time.
>
> The FBI had a simple message: The time for talk is over, we are moving in with tear gas, surrender now.
>
> The news was not well-received inside the compound where David Koresh and his followers had held forth under siege for 51 days. The line abruptly went dead . . .

For many years, sidebars and brights were the only outlets available to writers who wished to featurize news, but that situation would change quickly under the pressure of world events and electronic news media.

Contemporary alternatives

The sharp distinction between news and features began to erode during World War II as foreign correspondents attempted to explain the conflict and the complex events leading up to it. Faced with the task of making sense out of intricate military operations in a multinational theater, reporters were forced to move beyond a simple recounting of the facts of battle.

In an effort to convey the significance of what many of them were witnessing, correspondents set aside the inverted pyramid and began dispatches with a summary of their own analysis—as did the writer of this *New York Times* story in 1943:

ON THE TUNISIAN FRONT, Feb. 14 —
Reichsfuehrer Hitler cannot afford to lose one
battle in Tunisia. So narrow is the eastern
seacoast corridor that the Germans hold
between Field Marshall General Edwin
Rommel's position south of the Mareth line
and the Tunis-Bizerte area that the loss of one
battle would split the German forces.

Despite this and the Russian defeats, Herr
Hitler is rushing infantry by planes and ships
from Europe and it is obvious to those on the
spot that this North African campaign is
becoming a showdown rather than a sideshow
in the preparation for the attack on Europe.
To win, Herr Hitler's forces—under Marshall
Rommel, Col. Gen. Dietloff von Arnim
acting as a local commander in the north—
must, by one device or another, get more
elbow room by cracking through the line of
mountains nearest the sea.

This correspondent in the past twenty-four
hours has travelled from Medjez-el-Bab, our
position nearest Tunis, to Gafsa, an oasis on
the British First Army's southern flank. On
both sides patrol activities are grimmer . . .

The resulting story, as the above example indicates, provides real
insight into the news. From the standpoint of meaning, one story like
this equals any number of fragmentary accounts listing troop
movements, casualties, equipment losses, etc.

Although sporadic efforts were made after the war to apply these
techniques to public affairs reporting at home, the real impetus for
experimentation was the arrival of television with its own unique style
of electronic journalism. This new medium had the unique ability to
place viewers at the center of the news event and to provide them with
aural, visual and—according to at least one observer—even tactile
perception of its subjects. Scanning the television image, Marshall
McLuhan said, involves viewers in a "sensuous participation that is
profoundly kinetic and tactile, because tactility is the interplay of the
senses, rather than the isolated contact of skin and object."

However the nature of this experience is explained, one thing
seems indisputably clear: When compared to the rich sensory
experience offered by the TV image, the traditional newspaper page,

both in form and content, appeared static and dull. This fact, more than any other, accounts for the dramatic changes in print media that have occurred since the early 1960s.

THE "NEW GRAPHICS"

In an attempt to create a more dynamic format, daily newspapers reduced the number of columns from eight to six and switched to horizontal makeup systems that utilized fewer stories on a page. These efforts went hand in hand with increased concern for photographic display and a more sophisticated handling of typefaces. Added incentive for brightening the newspaper image came from the mechanical side, where advances in printing technology were outstripping the ability of the press to use them effectively.

One result of the renovation in graphics was a sharp reduction in the number of three- and four-paragraph stories that once cluttered newspaper pages. Short human interest items, like the page brighteners discussed earlier in this chapter, were gathered together and run in columns under a standing head. The emphasis on simplified layout with fewer page elements also created a demand for longer stories to run in horizontal blocks under multicolumn headlines.

Consequently, even though inverted pyramid stories continue to occupy a sizable portion of the news hole, more space than ever is allocated to interpretative news features, news analysis and investigative articles.

Daily newspapers have responded to the challenge of electronic media by ending the strict segregation of news and features, by giving writers greater leeway in the areas of interpretative reporting and stylistic innovation and by striving to upgrade graphic quality. The result is a newspaper that, while providing essential information, offers readers a more stimulating and visually satisfying experience.

FEATURIZED NEWS

The old system of dividing newspaper content into news and features was based on the prevailing practice of introducing hard news in inverted pyramid form before permitting it to become the subject of feature writing. The practice was a sound one because it prevented readers from missing important news hidden under feature leads.

Once radio and then television had clearly demonstrated their technological prowess in handling spot news, however, the older practice no longer had much logic to support it. If more and more newspaper readers were being introduced to important news by electronic media, why should newspapers merely repeat what most readers already knew? It took some time for newspaper editors to break old habits learned in a monopoly situation, but as the realities of the new media environment became apparent, editorial policies began to change.

How far those policies have changed can be gauged from this lead on a front-page story by Matt O'Connor and John O'Brien from the *Chicago Tribune:*

> Eight days ago, just outside the Dirksen Federal Building courtroom where a jury had been picked in her son's bank-robbery trial, Jeffrey Erickson's mother, June, pulled her son's attorney to the side.
>
> "Please tell the marshals Jeff is talking unusual," Richard Mottweiler recalled her saying. "I think he may try to make a run for it. He's looking around too much."
>
> "She just had a feeling," Mottweiler recalled Monday.
>
> After a lunch break, Mottweiler said he had a conference with the marshals and relayed June's concerns. "I told them upfront the possibility of something like this happening."
>
> On Monday, June Erickson's fears were realized. The man accused of being one half of a Bonnie and Clyde-style bank robbery team wrested a revolver away from a deputy U.S. marshal, fatally shot two men and then turned the gun on himself . . .

Such a lead on a news story of this magnitude would have been unthinkable only three decades ago. But editors today fully realize that most of their readers saw the videotapes of this carnage on the evening news the night before their story appeared. So instead of repeating yesterday's news, the *Tribune* added a new angle to the story: a prophetic warning from the killer's mother.

During the 1970s, newspapers began to experiment with featurized hard news stories and to include more short interpretative news features as well as feature-length analytical articles. Not all of the experimentation proved effective; occasionally, key information was buried under long, descriptive lead paragraphs—a style described by its critics as "Jell-O journalism." But in many cases the feature approach worked, producing stories that were far more interesting and enlightening than if they had been cast in strict inverted pyramid form.

That even a straightforward account of a criminal investigation can sometimes be enhanced by the use of a feature lead is shown in another *Chicago Tribune* story by Art Barnum:

> Paul Grgula, 31, of Glen Ellyn, thought he was stealing liquor when he took several bottles from a neighbor's apartment, Du Page County prosecutors said Friday.
>
> Then he offered drinks to his father and brother on New Year's Day, and, prosecutors said, it killed them.
>
> At first sheriff's detectives thought the substance consumed by Stephen Grgula, 65, and his son, Steven, 35, both of 22W100 McCormick Ave. in unincorporated Milton Township, was homemade liquor. But subsequent analysis has led some investigators to believe the substance was film-processing fluid, which usually has a cyanide base . . .

Although the experimentation of the 1970s and 1980s has subsided and newspapers generally have grown more conservative in handling hard news, the sharp division between news and features no longer exists. It has been replaced by an unbroken continuum of news styles ranging from the inverted pyramid story at one end to the human interest feature at the other. Today the terms "featurized news" or "news features" can be applied to any news story that uses feature elements to some degree. It would include what is essentially an inverted pyramid story with a feature lead as well as features that focus on the implications or significance of events.

The following story by Patrice Gaines-Carter from *The*

Washington Post illustrates the latter since it attempts to describe a *situation* rather than an event:

> Résumés are flying, tensions are high.
> The outward signs are subtle, but fear and loathing have arrived at city hall, where people are changing spending habits, eyeing each other suspiciously and sometimes railing against the mayor.
> Five thousand mid-level professionals know that as many as 2,000 city jobs paying at least $31,000 a year will be eliminated beginning as early as October. But they do not know which among them will get the dreaded pink slips, or who will use bumping rights to save themselves by snatching the job of a colleague.
> It doesn't help to know that the guy at the next desk already may have checked personnel records to determine whose job he might claim if his is one of those eliminated . . .

This kind of story could not have been written in inverted pyramid form, which requires well-defined events occurring in a narrow time frame, and it would not have appeared in a newspaper with a strict news-or-features policy.

While daily newspapers have retreated somewhat from featurizing hard news, use of the feature style on less weighty items is widespread and effective, as this lead from a (Baltimore) *Sun* story by Richard O'Mara testifies:

> LONDON — Yesterday was a bad day for Mr. Fox.
> And for Mr. Stag, Mr. Weasel, Mr. Hare and Mr. Hedgehog as well. But especially for Mr. Fox.
> The British Parliament, after a snarling five-hour debate, declined by 187–175 to extend to foxes and other wild mammals the same legal protections against cruelty that cover dogs and cats . . .

Had this story followed inverted pyramid style, it immediately would have lost half its interest and appeal.

The feature approach also works well on accounts of annual events that might otherwise produce repetitive stories from year to year. In the following example from the *Philadelphia Inquirer,* writer Edward Collimore uses a feature lead to give a fresh angle to a Memorial Day commemoration:

> They were remembered yesterday in the steady thump of marching feet on a macadam lane. In the clopping hooves of a riderless horse. In the haunting bagpipe strains of "Amazing Grace." And in the crack of musket volleys and a mournful bugle rendition of "Taps."
>
> John H. R. Storey, Robert T. Kelley and Pinkerton R. Vaughan may be unknown to most people—the unsung heroes of another time, whose only monuments are simple headstones in a forest of obelisks and statues at Laurel Hill Cemetery, along Kelly Drive.
>
> But their stories of courage were not forgotten by two dozen soldiers and patriots who honored them in graveside ceremonies as they commemorated the 125th anniversary of the traditional observance of Memorial Day, begun in 1868 as Decoration Day.
>
> Storey, Kelley and Vaughan were among 76 Philadelphia recipients of the Congressional Medal of Honor during the Civil War . . .

It is clear from the above examples how the application of feature techniques can add freshness and vitality to many kinds of news stories. Featurized news also offers daily newspapers a vehicle for providing readers with information not ordinarily seen on television. But if the liberal use of news features can enhance the competitive position of the daily press in relation to electronic media, it is an even more critical strategy for weeklies that must carve out a niche for themselves against radio, television and the dailies.

WEEKLY FEATURE STYLES

Although used frequently, the inverted pyramid is not a particularly helpful structure for weekly newspapers. Rarely do news events accommodate weekly publishing schedules so that stories can appear with a "yesterday" time tag in the lead. When a reporter applies the inverted pyramid to events that are several days old, the form only accentuates the story's age. Thus, if weekly newspapers wish to compete effectively with dailies, they must do two things: Offer information not available in the competing papers, and when offering the same information, do a better job of presenting it.

By using featurized news, weeklies can accomplish both goals at once. News features permit a weekly newspaper to take specialized or local news that received superficial treatment from the dailies, widen the perspective and produce a story with much more meaning and interest for the reader. To do that effectively, however, requires that weeklies abandon the inverted pyramid and develop a broad range of feature styles.

Today's most successful community and special interest weekly newspapers are doing just that. Since these publications have no need for a "today" or "yesterday" angle in their stories, they rarely use the inverted pyramid, except for brief items not reported in the daily press. Long interpretative articles and shorter topical stories are structured as features, with leads focused on significant or provocative aspects of the news rather than on a single action in a limited period of time.

Even when the story relates to an event that took place in the week prior to publication, the writer attempts to place the lead in a wider context—as did Carole Collins in the following example from the *National Catholic Reporter:*

> RIO DE JANEIRO, Brazil — It was the most critical of issues—survival of our planet. It was the worst of hot, humid weather.
>
> And measured by the difference in process and substance between official governmental deliberations and the participatory democracy of the Global Forum organized by nongovernmental organizations at the Earth Summit here last week, the battle over how to deal with the global ecological crisis has just begun.

The result is a more meaningful lead and a story that loses none of its importance by appearing several days after the event.

In some instances, weeklies simply ignore the "when" aspect altogether, as the *Maine Times* did in this story:

> Retirees may be as valuable for the Maine economy in coming years as defense spending, according to a new national study.
>
> Figures compiled by the State Policy Data Center show that direct federal payments to individuals—mainly Social Security and federal retirement and veterans' benefits— averaged $2,303 on a per capita basis in Maine in 1991, eighth highest in the country.

In longer articles, these weeklies use all of the feature writer's techniques: arresting leads, organic structure, vivid imagery, interesting quotes and strong endings. First-person stories are common and interviews occasionally take the form of question-and-answer reportage.

Since feature writing techniques will be discussed fully in Chapter 9, there is no need to describe them here. The following lead by Joy Zimmerman from the *Pacific Sun* in Marin County, California, shows how a weekly newspaper can use these techniques to draw readers into an important story:

> With a master's degree in public administration, 25 years of government service and extensive experience in program management and budget analysis, Eileen Siedman thought she know how to read a budget. That was before she encountered Marin's process.
>
> When Siedman retired in 1986 from her most recent job as an assistant inspector general of the U.S. Department of Commerce, she moved to Marin to be near her grown children. The last thing she wanted to do was analyze yet another public budget.
>
> Then several years ago, Siedman was introduced to a member of Marin Action, a citizen's group that had been studying Marin's budget process to see if it couldn't be improved. Asked if she would help out, Siedman hesitated, concerned that it might drain too much time and energy from her

other activities. On the other hand, she thought, how long could it take to do a thorough analysis of "this tiny little county of 250,000 that's about the size of a medium-sized city?"

Now, Siedman shakes her head in amazement at the amount of time she and other Marin Action folks have put into their effort—and, more to the point, how little response they've received from county officials...

When news can be presented with skill and understanding, as in the above examples, it loses its fragmentary character and becomes for the reader a rewarding source of information.

9 Writing the Feature Story

THE NEWSPAPER feature story has come of age. After serving for more than a half century as a diversion from the news, the feature story now is a journalistic form through which news can be given depth, meaning and perspective. No longer synonymous with soft news or entertainment and assigned to the back sections of the newspaper, features today share front-page space with the most important spot news stories.

Feature status underwent a transformation in the 1960s when editors realized that the feature offered newspapers a way of giving news the kind of depth and context often missing in electronic journalism. Feature writers turned away from the quaint personality and the offbeat scene to focus on newsworthy people and issues. Since then the use of features to analyze, interpret and background important issues has become standard procedure on most American newspapers.

The shift in the function of the feature is apparent in two examples from the *Philadelphia Inquirer.* The first, from 1938, is fairly typical of the period prior to the 1960s:

> Next to a bank, the worst place for passing a counterfeit coin is at the toll gate of the Delaware River Bridge.
>
> Last year $90.95 worth of patrons who tried it found that out, and this year $19.35 in bogus coins has been spotted by the vigilant toll collectors.
>
> Two reasons contribute to the almost 100 per cent efficiency of the uniformed men who take your quarters on the bridge, according to Ephraim Sharp, captain of the toll bureau.
>
> The first is constant handling of coins all day, every day, so that a quarter or half dollar that is the slightest bit "off" can readily be distinguished.
>
> "It has a greasy touch," Sharp explains.
>
> The second reason is that if a toll collector accepts a counterfeit, he has to make good the loss from his own pocket . . .

The second, a front-page story by *Inquirer* medical writer Donald C. Drake, indicates that by 1978 the feature played a much more serious role:

> Sitting in a darkened room, Dr. Sheila Moriber Katz focused the electron microscope until something that looked like a pebble popped eerily into the green, luminescent viewing field.
>
> "There! That's it," Dr. Katz said in a voice that betrayed awe. "After spending so much time looking for it, it's thrilling to see it there like that, almost held prisoner, so to speak."
>
> She moved the viewing field and smiled as more pebbles and other strange forms in the green glow caught her attention. She had become oblivious to the people standing around her in the darkness; she was lost in a microscopic world, entered by what she liked to think was astronomy in reverse.
>
> The pebbles that enraptured the shy, quiet-spoken pathologist at Hahnemann Medical College and Hospital were the bacteria that most scientists now believe cause "Legionnaires' disease" . . .

As the second example suggests, contemporary feature writing utilizes all of the traditional feature writing techniques—plus a few new ones—to report the news. The end product is a three-dimensional story that not only informs readers but provides them with a relevant context in which news takes on greater meaning and coherence.

Feature techniques

What sets off a well-written feature story from other types of newswriting is its structure. "Featurized" news stories may employ certain feature techniques, but the full-length feature goes the furthest in attempting to unify and connect its material.

Unlike the harsh geometry of the inverted pyramid story, feature structure is organic. It has a beginning, a middle and an ending, and all of the parts are closely related to each other. This means that before a writer can begin to write a feature, he or she must think about the story *as a whole*. It is a more difficult task than simply writing a good lead tied to a convenient "today" or "yesterday" peg. In features, the lead—whatever form it ultimately takes—derives from the writer's approach to the whole story.

Thus, before any thought can be given to constructing a compelling lead paragraph, the feature writer must step back from the material and attempt to find a theme or "angle" that will unify the article and generate reader interest. What the writer needs is—for lack of a better word—a thesis on which the entire article can be structured.

Some writers call this process "walking around the story." By this they mean that the writer, having reviewed the notes, must now relax and let the material suggest how it should be approached. Good story angles arise naturally from the data gathered on the subject, and it is the writer's task to explore the possibilities inherent in the material. When the material suggests two or more different approaches, the writer must decide which angle the audience would find most interesting.

In a feature on a widely known activist clergyman, Edward Power of the *Philadelphia Inquirer* chose this particular approach:

> On the outside, the Rev. David M. Gracie
> looks like a patrician preacher come to soothe
> a well-heeled flock.
>
> But no sooner does he start to talk of his
> recent trip to Honduras to help refugees from
> El Salvador than a different David Gracie
> emerges: urban revolutionary, labor activist,
> community organizer.
>
> Rebel priest.

Power decided to build the story on the contrast between Gracie's physical appearance and his radical political and social viewpoints, but he could have picked another angle. Gracie's father was a UAW official who worked for the Ford Motor Co., and Power might have decided to use as his theme Gracie's early exposure to labor conflict and its effect on his ministry.

The story angle, then, determines the final shape of the feature and what material will be included or left out. Because it is so crucial to the success of the feature, development of an effective angle should be given adequate time and thought. Once the angle has been selected, then—and only then—can writing begin in earnest. Now the writer can go back through his or her notes, looking for material to feature in the lead or in the ending, and generally attempting to determine how much information relates to the angle and whether any additional information might be necessary.

At this point, most feature writers will begin to draw up a rough outline of the topics in the order that they feel will provide maximum coherence for the article. Preliminary outlines, however, are tentative at best and subject to revision as new and better methods of organization evolve during the writing process itself.

Occasionally, a story angle will emerge early in the research stage. When this happens, writers can use it as a guide in gathering information, but they should not become so enamored of one approach that they refuse to discard it should a stronger, more effective angle turn up later.

FEATURE LEADS

Most feature stories develop out of information that is significant because of the wider perspective it brings to the news or the light it sheds on interesting personalities. At the same time, feature material usually lacks the sensational aspects of hard news. Consequently, the writer must employ a higher degree of skill in constructing a lead that will pull the reader strongly into the story. But in this task, feature writers—like their counterparts in fiction writing—also have a wider range of options at their disposal.

The writer may begin by using an anecdote, a snatch of dialogue, a paragraph of description, a direct quote, a narrative or a summary of the feature angle that highlights a provocative aspect of the story. In short, the only real test for an effective feature lead is that it works: It entices the unsuspecting reader into reading the story.

In a *Los Angeles Times* feature marking the 20th anniversary of the Woodstock music festival, writer Alan Parachini uses a narrative lead:

> WHITE LAKE, N.Y. — Walking tentatively, as if entering a shrine, four young men wandered into the large sloping hayfield on a little country lane called Hurd Road, a few miles from this Catskill Mountain village 90 miles northwest of New York City.
>
> Eventually, three of them sat down in the grass and chuckled as the fourth, a 16-year-old high school student, played the air as if it were a guitar, imitating the stereotyped choreography of rock bands.
>
> It is easy enough to find the hayfield, but it no longer has any resemblance to the form it took for three days in the late summer of 1969.

Boston Globe writer Gloria Negri chooses a direct quote that summarizes the story angle to introduce a feature on the economic problems of Pittsfield, Massachusetts:

> PITTSFIELD — At Mancy's Tonsorial Parlor on Melville Street, Frank Mancivalano has kept his finger on the pulse of his changing city—cutting hair, shaving faces and hearing rumor, gossip and fact for more than four decades.
>
> "I love this town," said Mancivalano, a barber for 42 of his 60 years. "But I'd sure like to see it moving again."

In a feature marking the 100th anniversary of Chicago's City News Bureau, Associated Press writer Sarah Nordgren opted for description:

> CHICAGO — In a cluttered downtown newsroom, City News Bureau reporters work the phones and listen to the police scanner, ears cocked for even the slightest suggestion of a story.
>
> The medical examiner's daily list of the dead is grist for the mill. An anonymous tip on a politician's daughter? Sirens in the Loop? Check it out.
>
> Check everything out. This is City News Bureau, inspiration and torchbearer of *The Front Page*, a gritty little wire service that is celebrating a century of rough and tumble journalism.

Philadelphia Inquirer writer David Johnson uses a play on words to introduce a feature timed to the opening of a Donald Trump casino in Atlantic City:

> ATLANTIC CITY — What hath gaud wrought?
>
> Today, Donald J. Trump opens his Taj Mahal Casino Resort, where, instead of faux marble and *Trump l'oeil* views, players will feel a virtual quarry's worth of real marble and see oh so many mirrors and windows— polishing them will require 110 gallons of concentrated cleaner each week.
>
> The Taj is a similitude of Trump, the rich kid from Queens who glories in nouveau riche architecture.

Another *Globe* news feature by Stephanie Simon uses an anecdotal approach to the problem of overworked medical interns:

> Dr. Adam Burrows has heard the horror stories: doctors falling asleep in the operating room or dozing during consultations.
>
> He has his own stories, too. Like the time he fell asleep on a patient's chest while

listening to a heartbeat or the time he and a fellow intern snoozed at a patient's bedside.

Chronic fatigue is part of the rite of passage that medical school graduates undergo during their three to five years as residents of training hospitals, when they may work up to 120 hours a week.

When more creative leads like the ones above are not available, feature writers can fall back on a summary lead. But even here interest can be heightened if an element of contrast, conflict, irony or paradox can be legitimately introduced.

Another *Inquirer* writer, Rich Henson, employs a summary lead but plays up the element of contrast:

By day, Robert Groden works in the laboratory of a Wayne photographic firm, performing specialized processes on photographs and films.

But give him a spare moment and his obsession takes over. The assassination of John F. Kennedy. Details. Details. Details. Groden can close his eyes and see all the details.

Even the most straightforward of summary leads becomes interesting with the help of skillful writing—as this example by Darren C. Hackett of *The Washington Post* demonstrates:

It has been used on the lawn of the White House, the flower beds of Constitution Gardens and the grounds of the governor's mansion in Annapolis. It has become a hot consumer product—dubbed by some gardening aficionados as the Dom Perignon of sludge.

ComPRO, as it is called, is genuine Montgomery County composted sludge, a recycled raw sewage product manufactured in Silver Spring by the Washington Suburban Sanitary Commission.

It is usually good practice to avoid direct address in writing leads. Beginners are likely to overuse this approach because it is easy, but starting out by addressing the reader seldom is as effective as a lead based on the creative use of story material. Similarly, asking questions in the lead that the reader can't answer creates frustration rather than interest.

While these are sound general rules, they can occasionally be broken to good effect if the reader has personal knowledge of the story's topic. The following direct-address lead on an Associated Press news feature by Robert Dvorchak is such a case:

> If you think more children than ever are being abused, if you think the rich are getting richer and the poor getting poorer, if you think health-care costs are more burdensome than ever—you're right.
>
> Sociologist Marc Miringoff has tracked 17 social problems for the last 20 years with his Index of Social Health, and after a steady decline its latest reading has sunk to its lowest point. In fact, the index has dropped 51 percent since numbers were first compiled in 1970.

Each of the above leads takes a wholly different approach to starting a feature, but all make it difficult for a reader—once he or she has read that far—to turn away from the story.

FEATURE DEVELOPMENT

Since feature writing does not follow the more confining "order of importance" of the basic news story, the writer does not face the problem of bridging gaps between unrelated topics that inverted pyramid writing often presents. Feature development, as noted earlier, is a more "organic" process in which related topics are kept together, making for greater coherence.

By the same token, the feature writer must hold to a higher standard of continuity. The abrupt shifts that occasionally are unavoidable in newswriting count as a weakness in the feature where the finished product should appear a seamless whole. But this requires of the writer a painstaking attention to detail, to the crafting of smooth transitions, to the rhythm of direct quotes and paraphrase, to the selection of anecdotal material and to the effective use of imagery—all of those techniques normally associated with the craft of fiction writing.

Transitions. Of all the above techniques, the ability to provide smooth transitions is paramount. Like a skilled cabinetmaker, the feature writer must assemble his or her material so that the joints do not show. Instead of using a transitional word or phrase to change the subject, as is often done in newswriting, the feature writer may need to construct a paragraph to shift the topic or to connect a lead to the story angle. Such a transitional, or "bridge," paragraph usually is required after a descriptive, narrative or anecdotal feature lead.

The opening of a story by Barry Yeoman in the *Independent Weekly* of Durham, North Carolina, contains a good example (italicized) of this kind of transition:

> With the flames growing nearer, Mary Bryant screamed as loud as she could. But on that September day in Hamlet, with her coworkers trying to flee, no one could hear her call. So she lowered her voice and directed it heavenward.
>
> "Lord, don't let me die in this place," she said. "Don't take me away from my children."
>
> *Those 15 whispered words have come to define the debate over workplace safety in North Carolina. This spring, in front of the state Legislative Building, Bryant's eyes welled up as she recounted the horror of the Imperial Foods blaze that killed 25 of her relatives and neighbors . . .*

The skillful use of transitions within a story persuades the reader that the writer's order is the most natural one. In a *Washington Post* feature on the city's Shiloh Baptist Church, writer Laura Sessions Stepp makes a graceful transition from the church's current expansion plans to its history:

> The question now is whether Shiloh can draw the new members it needs to sustain such an expansion. The Shaw neighborhood is rife with shootings and drugs. At

Pentecostal churches and mosques, African American membership is growing faster than at Baptist churches, and the number of black churchgoers under 30 is declining.

Shiloh's willingness to take such risks helps explain why it is one of the area's busiest and most visible urban churches.

Founded in 1864 by 20 freed slaves, it has been led by six preach-from-the-heels pastors and hundreds of energetic laypeople who believe that tutoring neighborhood children is as important as reading First Corinthians. Ten years ago, it built its ambitious Family Life Center, which offers more than 80 activities, including basketball and health clinics, math instruction and a restaurant.

A good transition must provide some kind of relationship between two different topics. If the writer takes the time to develop a coherent structure for his or her story, the task of creating smooth transitions should not be too difficult.

Quotations. Another key technique in feature development is blending direct quotes into the story in a way that keeps reader interest at a consistently high level. This goes beyond the technical aspects of handling direct quotes, as outlined in Chapter 5, and involves establishing a subtle rhythm between direct quotation and paraphrasing that adds variety and texture to the writing.

Too much paraphrasing or quoting at great length becomes monotonous to the reader; it is the skillful alternation from one to the other that heightens interest. In the feature on Father Gracie cited earlier, the writer demonstrates this technique:

Raised the son of a UAW official who worked for Ford Motor Co., Father Gracie said he knew early on that he wanted to work in the church. But he also sensed that work would take him into nontraditional areas such as the labor movement.

"One of my earliest memories," Father Gracie recalled, "is of Dad taking me by the hand to go to the plant and see the picket line. I remember seeing black men beating up

> white men. These were black men who had
> been imported as strikebreakers. I saw in that
> picket line how racial division could be
> exploited."
>
> His family's working-class background and
> his sense that workers were often targets for
> oppression convinced Father Gracie that
> unions—like churches—could be used to
> prevent such abuses.
>
> "I have been and always will be a partisan
> for organized labor," he said. "One reason is
> that I've always seen the labor movement as a
> force for unity among working people."

In newswriting, most direct quotes are selected primarily for their content, that is, to provide a verbatim rendering of an important or striking comment. In feature writing, however, quotes or dialogue containing little or no significant information may be used if they permit the writer to tell the story more vividly or to provide insight into the character of the subject.

In a *Denver Post* feature on former Colorado governor Bruce King, writer William Hart uses such a quote:

> Besides land and livestock, King said, his
> father also passed on to him a keen interest in
> Democratic politics. Bill King landed a
> political job as a highway road foreman—an
> especially prized position during the
> Depression—and got Gov. Clyde Tingley to
> attend the dedication of Stanley High School
> in 1935.
>
> "I was sitting in the audience when Gov.
> Tingley said that maybe one of us kids would
> grow up to be governor some day," King said.
> "I thought, 'Well, it might as well be me.'"

The above quote has no news value, but it gives the reader an insight into the character of the former governor.

Anecdotes. News features—especially those dealing with the technical aspects of government, politics or law—tend to become abstract unless the writer makes a concentrated effort to bring home the issues to the reader concretely. One of the most effective ways to do this is by frequently introducing anecdotal material to illustrate the key points of the story. To uncover such material, writers must constantly be on the lookout from the beginning of the research stage for interesting anecdotes, and they must ask subjects questions that elicit personal experiences related to the topic.

Frequent use of anecdotal material not only aids reader understanding but gives the story greater overall vitality. That anecdotes are likely to be the best remembered parts of the feature should be justification enough for their use.

In the story on Father Gracie cited above, the writer attempts to show how his subject acquired strong feelings about racial injustice, and he does so by using an anecdote:

> He tells a story about a black woman, Ethel Watkins, who had moved to the fringes of a white neighborhood. Soon, mobs of angry whites began showing up on her lawn to shout threats and obscenities. The polarization was such, Father Gracie recalled, that even police were reluctant to get involved.
>
> One Sunday, as he and Watkins sat in her home having lunch, he said, one of the mobs appeared.
>
> "They had gone to church and then had come to try to terrorize Ethel," Father Gracie recalled. "They showed up and here I was looking out at the white mob with Ethel. For the first time, I was looking at the world as they, black people, see it. That was a critical moment in my life. Since then I have refused to stop looking at the world that way."

Anecdotes are particularly useful in feature profiles where the writer wants to present a balanced picture of a controversial subject. By including quotes and anecdotal material from a variety of sources, the writer sets up, in effect, multiple camera positions from which a complex personality can be viewed in its entirety.

Description. Feature writers cannot lose sight of the fact that they use the print medium to communicate with readers who receive a major portion of their information via television, radio and film.

This means that today's newspaper reader has come to expect images as well as ideas. So strong are these expectations that few newspaper editors would consider running a feature story without at least one related photograph. But even a strong pictorial display does not let the writer off the hook. The writing itself must contain vivid images that permit the reader to see, hear and touch the subject.

In producing this kind of prose, writers are not trying to duplicate the work of electronic media. Their objective should be to provide readers with images that may be inaccessible to a reporter who must rely on a camera or microphone. The mere presence of microphones or a video camera can inhibit or alter the normal behavior of subjects, and both the format and economic structure of radio and television limit the extent to which their complex equipment can be deployed. Print media reporters, by contrast, enjoy almost unrestricted movement and, when necessary, can function as observers within a cloak of invisibility.

Thus, in turning to the feature, newspaper writers should exploit the peculiar advantages of their own medium, and they can do so with forceful descriptive writing that holds the reader with its texture and imagery. Beginners should be warned: Descriptive writing cannot serve as an excuse to depart from basic news style with its emphasis on brevity and on the key roles of noun and verb in sentence structure. Good description is achieved not by piling up adjectives but by including the kind of concrete details essential for pungent imagery.

In a *Philadelphia Inquirer* feature on the re-emergence of amusement piers at Atlantic City, writer William H. Sokolic describes one of the older piers:

> The last ride on Central Pier shut down in 1985. Today, several small shops front the Boardwalk, selling inexpensive clothing, souvenirs and fortunes. Except for the area used to store rolling chairs for the Shore Rolling Chair Co., the rest is a virtual ghost town. Cobwebs and chipping plaster cling tenaciously to vacant upstairs offices. Behind the ornate Boardwalk facade, the last vestige of the past—the rusting hulk of the space needle ride—towers over empty wooden planks.

By providing telling details, a writer enables the reader to see, hear and feel aspects of the scene being described. A generalized description short-circuits this process, leaving the reader with labels rather than images.

Effective feature development results from the skillful blending of all of the above techniques in a structure that appears—at least to the reader—to be the only appropriate one for that particular story. To produce such an effect, the writer must order the material coherently; experience weighs in heavily here, but even beginners can offset their handicap by making at least a rough outline of the topics to be covered in the order that seems most natural. This preliminary outline, as noted earlier, is always tentative—it will be revised often during the writing process—but without one the writer stands little chance of writing a coherent feature.

FEATURE ENDINGS

No other part of a feature distinguishes it so clearly from the typical inverted pyramid news story than its ending. Most news stories don't have endings—and for good reason! Stories with a functional ending cannot be shortened quickly by cutting from the bottom, as is often necessary in the fluid news environment of the daily press.

If feature stories resist rapid editing, they make up for this failing by having a longer shelf life; they can be used today, tomorrow or even next week without losing any of their interest or flavor. This characteristic directly results from the way the story is written. A feature story, as noted earlier in this chapter, is constructed organically with a beginning, middle and end—and the ending assumes almost as much importance as the beginning.

In a feature, the role of the ending is twofold: to restate the angle in a way that will leave a lasting impression on the reader, and to provide a clear, graceful finish to the story. While these may appear formidable criteria, they are not that difficult to satisfy because of the range of options available. As in constructing a lead, writers may use a direct quote, a segment of dialogue, an anecdote, a descriptive paragraph or—less often—a summary of the story angle.

In the *Los Angeles Times* feature on the 20th anniversary of Woodstock, the writer ends with a direct quote that reflects the feelings of many of the participants interviewed by the author:

> "It was more than just a party, but it *was* quite a party," he recalled of Woodstock. "It was the best weekend of my life. I felt kind of justified in the beliefs that I had . . . all that peace and love stuff.
>
> "I felt it was kind of a lesson we were trying to teach America that never really sank in."

In a *Boston Globe* feature on the city's trolley tour business, writer Robert Frank ends his story with this narrative:

> During a traffic jam, an orange trolley pulls up next to a blue trolley. One guide yells to the other, "Hey, when did you get out of detox?" After more name calling, the guides provoke their passengers into a shouting match, in order to prove which tourists are having more fun. One trolley's riders put on a weak show, and the conductor yells to his passengers, "You can do better than that!" The traffic starts moving again, and the defeated car rolls off in silence.

St. Petersburg Times writer Chris Lavin uses an anecdotal ending to close out a humorous feature on residents of Florida's Marion County who are contesting each other's claims to Indian ancestry:

> Lathel Duffield, an anthropologist in the bureau's acknowledgement office, says there are many Americans, some who may even have a distant Indian ancestor, who come to admire the Indian traditions so much they believe they and others like them should be recognized as true Indians.
>
> Duffield, who is a Cherokee, says true Indian tribe members have a name for these people:
>
> "We call them Wannabees."

Since the reader at this point knows the implications of the story, the writer can freely select material for an ending—such as an impressionistic paragraph or emotional quote—that would have been unsuitable for the lead.

Sheryl James, another *St. Petersburg Times* writer, chooses such an ending for her feature on Don West, an 82-year-old radical and former labor activist:

> The man from Meals on Wheels stops by with two Styrofoam containers of food. He asks in a booming, friendly voice, "Got any more of those papayas?"
>
> There are papayas and bees in the back yard. Honey. West walks slowly outside and opens the high wood fence that is hardly any taller than his 6-feet-3 frame, and fetches the man some papayas. The grass is scruffy. Florida is flat and warm, and it looks like rain.

Beginning feature writers should understand that endings are constructed by putting certain material at the end, not by tacking on a moral or editorial comment about the story.

Forms of the feature

Any writing form as open to creativity and invention as the feature story resists neat division into categories. Add to this two decades of journalistic experimentation, and the attempt to place labels on features becomes a questionable—if not futile—exercise.

Techniques once reserved for human interest stories now are applied to the news, while investigatory skills and painstaking reporting have become a prerequisite for contemporary feature writing. Reportorial judgment plays a vital role in both news and features, and the first-person story—once a newsroom taboo—regularly appears in dailies as well as weeklies. In short, the old lines that divided news from features and one kind of feature from another have been all but erased by innovation.

From the writer's point of view, the only useful distinction that can be made is one that separates features related to the news from those which are not. Consequently, in terms of technique, there are only two basic types: news features and human interest features, and even these are not mutually exclusive. Though imprecise, the distinction serves a purpose by highlighting certain characteristics common to each category, which will be examined next. Since personal profiles, whether they fall in the news or human interest category, have several requirements of their own, they will be discussed in a separate section.

THE NEWS FEATURE

The term "news feature" can be applied to almost any feature writing that relates to a news event. It would include news analyses, stories highlighting trends, and interpretative articles that try to explain events and predict their consequences. It may also describe investigative features that, by exposing conditions about which the public was unaware, "make news."

Good news features combine vigorous and imaginative writing coupled with careful research and a concern for factual accuracy. Since features are designed to offer readers a more meaningful context for news, writers should bring informed judgments to bear on the story.

Because of its unique ability to put events in a wider perspective, the news feature has become the most common story form in regional and national weekly newspapers that have emerged in response to electronic journalism. An interpretative feature remains timely for a relatively long period, and, in the hands of an experienced and observant reporter, can provide insights and understanding unobtainable in any other medium.

News feature style varies considerably along a spectrum that ranges from news analysis—only a few steps removed from straight reporting—at one end, to descriptive, emotionally charged accounts of news events, at the other. While the former rely primarily on the writer's critical judgment and the latter on narrative technique and vivid imagery, most news features fall somewhere in between and employ elements of both.

A good example of news analysis is the following story by D'Vera Cohn and Richard Morin of *The Washington Post,* revealing the implications of the 1990 Census figures for the District of Columbia:

The dispersion of blacks, Asians and Hispanics throughout the Washington area in the 1980s has reduced the proportion of overwhelmingly white neighborhoods, according to a Washington Post analysis of 1990 Census figures.

From the dockside villas of Annapolis to the new town houses in Loudon County, however, substantial racial segregation persists, especially in the black inner city. And growing diversity often has brought tension, violence or white flight.

Overall, census figures show that blacks, whites and Asians are more evenly spread through the area than a decade ago. Hispanics, following the pattern of earlier immigrant groups, are more isolated in ethnic enclaves than in 1980 . . .

At the opposite end of the spectrum stands the news feature that gives a human dimension to the news. This one by Fen Montaigne of the *Philadelphia Inquirer* was part of a series describing life in the Soviet Union:

LENINGRAD — Forgive Alexandra Vasiliyevna Bauman her nonchalance.

But for a woman who has lived through World War I, the Russian Revolution, the German siege of Leningrad, the rest of World War II and the Stalin years, the country's current travails are, well, no big deal.

Bauman is 91 now, and she measures out her life in kopeks and small pleasures. She subsists on 150 rubles—$88—a month, and by most definitions lives in poverty. Somehow she makes it look anything like that.

She lives in the same high-ceilinged apartment that she moved into as a bride in 1924. It has lovely family antiques, and no hot water. She makes do with a trip to the public baths twice a month.

Bauman eats spartan meals of porridge, barley soup and black bread off old, chipped china. She enjoys meat a few times a week. Vegetables generally come in the form of potatoes, onions and carrots.

> But for someone who lived on grass and
> wallpaper paste during the Leningrad siege,
> her current fare is not bad . . .

The most comprehensive form of the news feature is, of course, the investigative series. In preparing a series, the writer sets out to explore a news topic and to report on the findings, usually in from three to six installments. A series may originate with a directive from an editor to investigate a subject of current interest, or it may arise spontaneously when a reporter seeking information for a single article finds himself or herself in the middle of a much larger story that deserves full series treatment.

Although it may be based on extensive research and possibly even statistical analysis, series writing cannot afford to be dull or technical without losing many potential readers. To make the research come alive, writers must use all appropriate feature techniques.

In a two-part series on the high cost of aging, Michael Clements of *The Detroit News* Washington Bureau used this lead on his first article:

> Martha Louise Bowles spent more than 50 of her 82 years in East Detroit, raising her family and playing by society's rules of thrift and saving for old age.
>
> But less than six months at a $110-a-day nursing home in Warren exhausted her modest $18,000 nest egg, leaving her dependent on Medicaid health benefits for the poor. When Bowles was hospitalized last month for a broken hip, her nursing home gave her bed to someone else.
>
> Like many of Michigan's 50,000 nursing home residents, Bowles and her family have discovered what may be life's last cruel reversal of fortune: Unless you're rich enough to afford top-quality care in a private nursing home, you may need to go broke to qualify for care that is second best.

Each installment in a series should be treated as a separate article. Thus, in dividing the overall topic into installments, writers must make sure that each division can support a fully developed feature with its own story angle. While installments may vary in style depending on what aspect of the topic is under consideration, the series as a whole must exhibit a generally consistent tone and strong continuity. To maintain continuity, writers should include enough information from previous articles to make the current installment understandable to readers.

Expansion of the news feature in all of its forms is the most significant development in newswriting since the rise of electronic journalism. Consequently, the ability to write interesting news features is an important skill for print journalists who hope to advance in their profession.

HUMAN INTEREST STORIES

Despite the current dominance of the news feature, human interest stories are not obsolete. As long as newspapers exist, there will be a place for articles designed only to move the reader by their pathos, humor or gentle revelations of the human spirit.

While human interest occupies a less prominent position than it once did in feature writing, its role remains vital. Now that feature writers have joined general assignment reporters in the pursuit of significant news, there is an even greater need for stories that offer some contrast to the general preoccupation with serious themes.

A well-written human interest feature reminds the reader that individual human beings and small events still can move and teach us by their example. But it takes a perceptive writer to discover these subjects beneath the rush of important events.

Some human interest features, like the following one by Cynthia Hubert of the *Des Moines Register,* force the reader to stop for a moment and look at ordinary events in a different way:

> AMES, Ia. — Dawn Nelson is here because she loves animals.
>
> For the next three days, she will listen to lectures about how their bodies work, how they react to pain, how they experience fear. She will examine a scruffy gray tomcat and a striped kitten small enough to fit into the palm of her hand. She will talk to them in a soft, calming voice and gain their trust. She will scratch their ears and gently stroke their

fur.

Then she will kill them.

Welcome to Euthanasia School, a course that veterinarian Ronald Grier wishes did not have to exist . . .

Others single out the offbeat or unusual, as does this story by Jay Searcy in the *Philadelphia Inquirer:*

HERMITAGE, Pa. — Shhhh. Quiet please.

They're about to tee off here at Dum Dum, which may be the only free golf course in the United States, even the world.

It is 7:55 on a weekday morning, and in the gravel parking lot across the street are three cars, a bread truck, a van from Ohio and a woman in a pickup truck with a load of 12-year-old boys.

They say people come here to play from as far away as Japan—not because it is grand or challenging, but because they don't believe a free golf course really exists . . .

Lacking a news connection as a built-in attention factor, the human interest feature demands a high level of writing skill. To absorb readers in stories of obscure personalities or unusual places, the writer must offer fresh insights, vivid imagery, interesting quotes and language that is free of clichés and stereotypes. To accomplish this is no easy task, but the writer who can turn out human interest features that make readers pause and reflect—even momentarily—on the hidden talent, wisdom and beauty that surround them, is an asset to any newspaper staff.

PERSONAL PROFILES

The personal profile is a feature that aims to acquaint the reader with the personality of another individual. If the subject is significant because of a connection with a news event, the profile becomes a news feature; if the subject's significance stems from qualities perceived by the writer, the profile is considered a human interest feature.

In either case, the writer attempts, through the medium of print, to create a three-dimensional portrait of a human being. This portrait will not be a painting, complete in every detail, but a sketch that—regardless of its size—captures the spirit of the subject in relatively few strokes.

Personal profiles have always been a popular form of the feature. But the power of television to bring viewers into intimate contact with its subjects has put added pressure on print media to approximate this intimacy within the confines of type and photography. The feature profile enables print journalists to acquaint readers with significant personalities who are beyond the range of the video camera.

Whether applied to news or human interest features, the techniques for creating vivid profiles remain essentially the same. They include the use of descriptive details that help the reader to visualize the subject's physical appearance; direct quotes that reveal the subject's views, character and speech patterns; and anecdotes that illustrate the subject's experience.

From the standpoint of technique, the difference between news and human interest profiles is mainly one of emphasis. When subjects are chosen because of their connection to the news, the reader naturally expects to find this relationship highlighted in the story. Accordingly, the writer gives priority to quotes and background information related to the news event at the expense of physical description and anecdotal material that would be included in human interest profiles. Yet for a news profile to hold the interest of readers conditioned by electronic media, it must contain all of these elements to some degree.

Descriptive writing is most effective when it is woven tightly into the narrative, as in this paragraph from a profile of Dr. Jonas Rappeport, a widely known forensic psychiatrist, by Michael Ollove of *The* (Baltimore) *Sun:*

> Dr. Rappeport sits at a conference table in his cluttered office surrounded by four psychiatrists who want to follow him into forensic psychiatry. He is a small man with square, large-framed glasses that dominate his oval face and an unexpectedly booming voice to which the others are paying strict attention. But today he is not lecturing, only prodding them with questions.

A description of the subject's physical environment also heightens the reader's visual awareness. In a human interest profile of Benny McCrary, who with his brother once held the world record for the heaviest set of twins, *Atlanta Constitution* writer Rebecca McCarthy provides both a physical description of her slimmed-down subject and the stage setting for the interview:

> He sits at a table in Shufford's Country Store, a flea market-warehouse flung beside the railroad tracks in Arden, 20 miles north of Hendersonville. He wears tinted glasses, a small mustache, jeans and a plaid sports shirt. His face is slim, the skin smooth but for a slight bulge of chewing tobacco. His cheekbones and collarbone are pronounced.
>
> "This is all skin," he says, grabbing the inside of his thighs. "My doctor says if I have cosmetic surgery and have this removed, I'll lose another 60 or 70 pounds. But that ain't cheap. It'll cost 15 grand."
>
> He reaches for the Styrofoam cup on the table and discreetly spits . . . .
>
> Near his table are a few pinball machines and a snack bar of the shiny yellow metal seen in carnivals. To the right are display cases of jewelry and shelves filled with ceramic birds, plastic flowers, windup toys, Christmas decorations, funeral wreaths and clothes.

The *St. Petersburg Times* profile of Don West, cited earlier in this chapter, focused primarily on his activities as a labor activist, but it also included a direct quote that revealed West the man:

> "I've never taken a man to court in my life, and I don't intend to. And neither do I spend any time defending myself when I'm attacked. If my life can't speak for me, then I think my tongue's a pretty feeble instrument to defend myself with."

Revelatory quotes like these add an extra dimension to feature profiles, as do anecdotes, which are particularly effective for dramatizing a subject's experiences. In the *Philadelphia Inquirer* feature on a 91-year-old Russian woman cited earlier, the writer wishes to show how harsh life was during the siege of Leningrad in World War II and uses an anecdote effectively:

> Her brother died at the front, her father perished from starvation, and she had no idea of the fate of her son, evacuated from the city in 1941. One day in late 1944, after the siege was lifted, there was a knock on the door of her sister's apartment, where Bauman was living. Bauman opened the door and saw a gaunt teenage boy, who asked for Bauman's sister.
>
> "I called her," said Bauman, crying as she recalled the incident, "and she came and yelled at me when she saw him. 'Can't you recognize your own son?'"
>
> Bauman and her son failed to recognize each other because they were both so emaciated.

If physical description, revelatory quotes and anecdotal material add life to news profiles, they are even more essential to human interest articles where the writer must justify the subject's importance by the quality of the writing. Obtaining this material in sufficient quantity for a well-developed story, then, is a prerequisite for profile writing. No matter how well he or she can write, a reporter without basic skills in interviewing will be handicapped when it comes to turning out strong personal features. Thus, a few suggestions are in order about the conduct of interviews.

It is axiomatic that success in interviewing is directly proportional to the reporter's preparation for the interview. This means that the reporter should try to find out as much as possible about the subject in advance of their meeting. Newspaper clipping files, biographical references and encyclopedia articles about the topic—all may prove useful sources of this information. Before interviewing an author, a reporter should also review the subject's writings.

With this preliminary research completed, the reporter should draw up a list of questions that will likely elicit significant comments from the subject. The importance of this list cannot be overstressed. Without it, the reporter will come away from the interview with missing information.

In the interview itself, the reporter must establish rapport with the subject. Many experienced interviewers begin by talking about subjects unrelated to the key areas of the interview and bring out their notebooks only when the initial awkwardness has been overcome. The reporter's manner should be pleasant and not antagonistic, but intelligent questions which indicate that the interviewer has done his or her homework, coupled with an obvious concern for accuracy, will do most to gain the confidence of the subject.

Finally, the reporter must maintain effective control of the interview. When the subject drifts away to areas irrelevant to the story, the interviewer must steer the conversation gently but firmly back to the key topics. At the same time the reporter must remain alert for unexpected material of importance and pursue it by further questioning. In summary, the skillful interviewer is an active, creative agent in the interview process—asking questions, taking notes, guiding conversation—but all the while listening for colorful or revealing comments and observing the physical characteristics of the subject.

Among all forms of the feature—news and human interest—the personal profile continues to dominate. This is not surprising since it offers the reader an intimate glimpse of another human being and the journalist a showcase for the most sophisticated writing skills.

In this chapter—and in the eight preceding it—the basic skills involved in writing news and feature stories have been outlined. Mastering these skills, however, is just the first step in the process of becoming a professional journalist. Once beginning journalists develop some proficiency in writing news, they must learn the techniques for gathering it—especially from sources that often are not easily accessible nor overly cooperative.

The quickest way for beginners to hone writing and reporting skills is to find a place where they can practice them under actual newspaper conditions. Student newspapers offer an excellent starting point, as do weekly newspapers and suburban sections of daily newspapers, which often hire college students and others as stringers to cover municipal meetings. Many dailies buy feature stories on a freelance basis, offering beginners an opportunity to break into print by exploring local topics in an interesting and meaningful way. Similar opportunities exist at ethnic, special interest and trade publications.

All of this is a roundabout way of saying that without some kind of experience to complement it, journalism instruction becomes about as effective as swimming lessons in a classroom. Sooner or later, the prospective journalist must take the plunge. If this brief guide to newswriting has served the reader as a springboard, the author will be more than satisfied.

Suggested Reading

The following titles are recommended to readers who wish to continue their study of journalistic writing beyond the limits of this guide.

Associated Press Stylebook and Libel Manual. 3d ed. Reading, Mass.: Addison-Wesley Publishing Co., Inc., 1993.

Berner, R. Thomas. *Language Skills for Journalists.* 2d ed. Boston: Houghton Mifflin, 1984.

Bernstein, Theodore M. *The Careful Writer: A Modern Guide to English Usage.* New York: Athenaeum, 1977.

_____. *Watch Your Language.* New York: Pocket Books, 1965.

Bremner, John. *Words on Words: A Dictionary for Writers and Others Who Care About Words.* New York: Columbia University Press, 1980.

Brooks, Brian S., and James L. Pinson. *Working With Words: A Concise Handbook for Media Writers and Editors.* 2d ed. New York: St. Martin's Press, 1993.

Brooks, Terri. *Words' Worth: A Handbook on Writing and Selling Nonfiction.* New York: St. Martin's Press, 1989.

Cappon, Rene J. *Associated Press Guide to News Writing.* 2d ed. New York: Prentice Hall, 1991.

Flesch, Rudolph. *The ABC of Style.* New York: Harper & Row, 1964.

_____. *The Art of Readable Writing.* rev. ed. New York: Collier Books, 1986.

Kennedy, George, Darryl R. Moen, and Don Ranly. *The Writing Book.* Englewood Cliffs, N.J.: Prentice-Hall, 1984.

Kessler, Lauren, and Duncan McDonald. *When Words Collide: A Journalist's Guide to Grammar and Style.* 3d ed. Belmont, Calif.: Wadsworth Publishing Co., 1992.

Schertzer, Margaret. *The Elements of Grammar.* New York: Collier Books, 1986.

Strunk, William, Jr., and E. B. White. *The Elements of Style.* 3d ed. New York: Macmillan, 1979.

United Press International Stylebook. 3d ed. Lincolnwood, Ill.: National Textbook Co., 1992.

Zinsser, William. *On Writing Well: An Informal Guide to Writing Nonfiction.* 4th ed. New York: Harper & Row, 1990.

INDEX